Betsy Webb

HAWKS
and
OWLS
of North America

HAWKS and OWLS

of North America

A Complete Guide to North American Birds of Prey

Donald S. Heintzelman

Universe Books
New York

Published in the United States of America in 1979
by Universe Books
381 Park Avenue South, New York, N.Y. 10016

© 1979 by Donald S. Heintzelman

Library of Congress Catalog Card Number: 78-65623
ISBN 0-87663-335-1

Printed in the United States of America

CONTENTS

ILLUSTRATIONS

Illustrations

Except as otherwise indicated, all photographs were taken by Donald S. Heintzelman.

PREFACE

I have written this book for students, birders, ecologists, conservationists, and raptor enthusiasts at less than professional level.. It is *not* my intent for the book to be a source of original information, although in a few places such information appears. Rather, I wanted to provide for a general reading audience a broad picture of North American birds of prey in which important aspects of their lives are discussed. Besides hawks and owls, vultures, kites, eagles, Ospreys, caracaras and falcons are included in this broad view.

Several books now in print discuss some aspects of the life histories of North American birds of prey, but many current topics are not touched upon in those works. Unquestionably the large two-volume work *Eagles, Hawks and Falcons of the World* by Leslie Brown and Dean Amadon will remain a standard reference on the diurnal birds of prey for many years. However, its high cost and large size make it more of a professional reference than a book intended for popular use, and it does not cover owls. In a somewhat similar manner the two volumes on the life histories of North American birds of prey by Arthur Cleveland Bent remain classics but are badly outdated in many respects and do not treat such topics as pesticides, captive breeding of raptors, and related issues of today. Nevertheless they still are important volumes and worth owning.

During the past century a number of excellent books and booklets have appeared dealing with the hawks and owls of North

America. Many were issued by government agencies. Others were published by private conservation organizations. Still others appeared under the imprints of university presses and commercial publishers.

Among the books I consulted, in addition to my own *The Hawks of New Jersey, Autumn Hawk Flights,* and *A Guide to Eastern Hawk Watching,* are the American Birding Association's *A.B.A. Checklist: Birds of Continental United States and Canada,* American Ornithologists' Union's *Check-List of North American Birds* (Fifth Edition and supplements), Austing's *The World of the Red-tailed Hawk,* Austing and Holt's *The World of the Great Horned Owl,* Bailey's *The Raptorial Birds of Iowa,* Bent's *Life Histories of North American Birds of Prey,* Bijleveld's *Birds of Prey in Europe,* Broun's *Hawks Aloft: The Story of Hawk Mountain,* Brown's *African Birds of Prey,* Brown and Amadon's *Eagles, Hawks and Falcons of the World,* Choate's *The Dictionary of American Bird Names,* Craighead and Craighead's *Hawks, Owls and Wildlife,* Fisher's *The Hawks and Owls of the United States in their Relation to Agriculture,* Gabrielson and Lincoln's *Birds of Alaska,* Greenway's *Extinct and Vanishing Birds of the World,* Grossman and Hamlet's *Birds of Prey of the World,* Hamerstrom's *Birds of Prey of Wisconsin,* Hausman's *The Hawks of New Jersey and their Relation to Agriculture* and *Birds of Prey of Northeastern North America,* Hickey's *Peregrine Falcon Populations,* Koford's *The California Condor,* May's *The Hawks of North America,* McDowell and Luttringer's *Pennsylvania Birds of Prey,* Oberholser's *The Bird Life of Texas,* Phillips, Marshall, and Monson's *The Birds of Arizona,* Phillips and Kirkpatrick's *Hawks and Owls of Indiana,* Spofford's *The Golden Eagle in the Trans-Pecos and Edwards Plateau of Texas,* Sprunt's *North American Birds of Prey,* Stone's *Bird Studies at Old Cape May,* Van Tyne and Berger's *Fundamentals of Ornithology,* and Wilbur's *The California Condor, 1966-76: A Look at its Past and Future.*

A considerable amount of information also was extracted from the ornithological periodical literature, especially from *American Birds, American Midland Naturalist, Annals Carnegie Museum, Atlantic Naturalist, Audubon, Auk, Birding, Bird-Lore, Cassinia, Chesapeake Science, Condor, Dissertation Abstracts International, EBBA News, Frontiers, Jack-Pine Warbler, Journal of Wildlife Management, Living Bird, Nature, Oriole, Pennsylvania Game News, Science, Search,* and *Wilson Bulletin.*

A portion of chapter 2 dealing with the Black Vulture is adapted from my article "The Black Vulture in Pennsylvania" appearing in the May 1969 issue of *Pennsylvania Game News* and is used with the permission of the Pennsylvania Game Commission.

Part of chapter 7 dealing with the Osprey is loosely adapted from my article "The Ospreys of Cedar Island" published in the April 1972 issue of *Frontiers* published by the Academy of Natural Sciences of Philadelphia and is used with the permission of that institution.

Parts of chapters 11, 14, and 15 are very loosely adapted from (and greatly expanded upon) *The Hawks of New Jersey* with the permission of the New Jersey State Museum.

A portion of chapter 12 is adapted, in part, from my article "Autumn Hawk Watch" published in the October 1970 issue of *Frontiers* published by the Academy of Natural Sciences of Philadelphia and is used with the permission of that institution. Additional portions of chapter 12 are loosely based upon some information contained in *Autumn Hawk Flights* (Rutgers University Press, 1975) and *A Guide to Eastern Hawk Watching* (Pennsylvania State University Press, 1976).

In developing many portions of this book I relied heavily upon my own field experience with birds of prey extending over a period of a quarter of a century. During this time countless discussions with other raptor enthusiasts provided a wide spectrum of points of view regarding many raptor issues. These background discussions also were helpful as I wrote this book.

Photographs add a great deal of interest and value to this book and I used my own whenever possible. Additional photographs were provided by various agencies and individuals, including the National Park Service, United States Fish and Wildlife Service, the White House, and Allan D. and Helen Cruickshank, Harry Goldman, Heinz Meng, M. Alan Jenkins, Richard Pough, Ron Quigley, Jan Sosik, Fred Tilly, and Sanford R. Wilbur.

A few additional illustrations or quotations are reprinted with the permission of the editors of the *Auk, Condor, Journal of Wildlife Management,* and the *Wilson Bulletin.*

1

INTRODUCTION

From the beginning of recorded history, and probably for millennia prior to that, man has been fascinated and inspired by hawks and owls. Large and powerful, these splendid birds symbolized a degree of airborne freedom which man seemingly never could achieve.

During the splendor of the ancient Egyptian civilization, both a vulture and a falcon served as deities. One of the falcon gods was named Horus. Later, across the waters of the Mediterranean, the Golden Eagle appeared on many Roman objects and symbolized the power and majesty of the Roman Empire. In ancient Athens an owl appeared on the city's coins, the symbol of Athena, the Goddess of Wisdom, for whom the city was named. Centuries later, during the Middle Ages, all classes of society from serf to king and emperor participated in the sport of hawking or falconry—an activity whose roots extend 4,000 years or more into the history of Asian peoples.

In North America birds of prey also were equally important as symbols of power, freedom, and good fortune in the lives of American Indians. Kwakiutl Indians of the Pacific Northwest fashioned dance costumes after eagle-like images. In the Midwest feathers from eagles were used to decorate the dress of important Indians. There even is evidence that the legendary thunderbird may have been a gigantic, nearly extinct condor-like vulture with a wingspread of 16 or 17 feet, *Teratornis incredibilis*. Such a bird probably made considerable noise when flying and landing, thus adding credence to the Indian legend.

5

The Bald Eagle, the national bird, is shown on the Seal of the United States of America. Photo courtesy of The White House.

When the American colonists declared their independence from Great Britain, the leaders of the new United States were faced with the task of selecting a national bird. Benjamin Franklin pressed for the selection of a "respectable" bird, the Wild Turkey. Most of his colleagues, however, preferred the Bald Eagle as the national bird of the United States of America. This was an appropriate choice. This splendid eagle truly is an American species. However, its future survival is seriously threatened by DDT and other pesticide pollution which contaminated the food chains of eagles and certain other raptors. Eagles deposited eggs with thin shells which broke unusually easily. The result? Very few Bald Eagles reared young for more than a decade, and the species almost became extinct because young birds were not produced to replace older eagles which died. Fortunately the use of DDT now is banned in the

United States, and it appears that the eagles eventually will recover some of their former numbers although this will not happen for many years. We do not yet know if the Peregrine Falcon will recover, but efforts are under way to try to save these spectacular birds. Full details are discussed later in this book.

Today ecologically informed people understand and appreciate the importance of predators, including hawks and owls. They strongly support conservation regulations which protect these valuable and exciting animals.

In earlier years, however, raptors were poorly understood and frequently were destroyed. For example, in Pennsylvania hatred for hawks and owls was widespread and reached great intensity during the latter part of the last century when the state legislature enacted the infamous Scalp Act of 1885. It placed a bounty on the lives of many predatory mammals and all hawks and owls except the Barn Owl, Screech Owl, and Saw-whet Owl. Fifty cents was paid for each hawk or owl killed and brought to an appropriate official of the county in which the bird was taken. The result was devastating. Before the bounty was revoked several years later, at least $150,000 was paid in claims. At least one-half of that amount went for

In 1932 these hawks were shot at what is now Hawk Mountain Sanctuary in eastern Pennsylvania. Photo by Richard H. Pough.

raptors. Yet the system failed as do all bounty systems, because they create unbalanced environments.

The Scalp Act should have been a vivid and informative lesson in the foolishness of trying to "control" ecologically necessary and valuable predators. But it was not. In 1929 authorities in Pennsylvania again placed a five-dollar bounty on Northern Goshawks, Great Horned Owls, and various other predators. These wasteful payments continued for more than 30 years. The result was a needless waste of money and wildlife. A table shows the number of Great Horned Owls killed and submitted for bounty payments to the Pennsylvania Game Commission during the years 1947 through 1962.

Table of Great Horned Owls Killed for Bounty in Pennsylvania	
FISCAL YEAR	NUMBER KILLED
1947-48	1,429
1948-49	1,836
1949-50	1,942
1950-51	1,477
1951-52	1,714
1952-53	1,688
1953-54	1,237
1954-55	1,233
1955-56	1,091
1956-57	1,234
1957-58	1,115
1958-59	1,047
1959-60	1,103
1960-61	1,222
1961-62	1,406

Early in this century hawk shooting became extremely popular. Countless thousands of hawks were slaughtered during migration at various concentration points. However, in 1934, the shooting was stopped at Hawk Mountain, Pennsylvania, when conservationists purchased the mountain and created the well known wildlife sanctuary now there. It was the first sanctuary for birds of prey in the world. But elsewhere along Pennsylvania's hawk ridges the slaughter continued unabated during autumn for another 22 years. Nobody can estimate the number of hawks which were killed during those years. The number must be staggering. And, as

This Red-tailed Hawk was shot in the 1950's at a shooting site near Hawk Mountain. The bird suffered a shattered wing and was kept in captivity at Hawk Mountain for many years where it was exhibited to the public.

recently as 1971, Americans were shocked to learn of the illegal slaughter of over 700 Golden Eagles from airplanes in the western United States by sheep ranchers. Indeed, in another more recent case in Texas, several ranchers were caught as they carried out an illegal effort to kill hundreds of eagles. Some badly informed people still hate birds of prey and kill them illegally when opportunities occur.

Dead hawks, shot illegally in 1956 near Bake Oven Knob, Pa., include an Osprey (center), a Northern Harrier (bottom left), a Peregrine Falcon (bottom right), and eight Broad-winged Hawks. The Peregrine Falcon now is an endangered species in North America.

Despite the tragic loss of these raptors, more and more people now understand the ecological roles of birds of prey in the natural world and want these birds protected. Thus, in 1972, the United States of America signed an international treaty with Mexico providing full federal protection for all birds of prey. Such protective measures now are essential to raptor conservation because many species are declining in numbers at an alarming rate and a few are on the brink of extinction. Unfortunately, at the very time when raptors should be left in the wild to carry out their vital ecological roles in helping to maintain the balance of nature, falconry is becoming increasingly popular in the United States and Canada. Many birds of prey are being captured and removed from the natural environment by people who look on falconry as good sport. It is to be hoped that this needless activity, very damaging to the future of falcons, will be banned.

Hawks and owls have practical values to people aside from their basic ecological roles. They are sensitive biological indicators reflecting environmental pollution and habitat destruction. Thus birds of prey are related to our welfare even when we may be unaware of their importance.

Finally, it is necessary to consider briefly the relationships of hawks with owls. Earlier ornithologists thought that these birds were closely related to each other because of their predatory habits and similar external features such as strong feet with talons and hooked bills designed for tearing flesh. Therefore all birds of prey were placed together in one group. Today, however, with more information available, we know that hawks and owls resemble each other only superficially. They are not closely related to each other from an evolutionary viewpoint. Indeed, hawks and owls evolved quite separately from each other. The diurnal birds of prey, the hawks and their relatives, all belong to the order Falconiformes. In contrast, the owls all are placed in another group, the order Strigiformes. It is only because of their similar predatory behavior that hawks and owls are discussed together in one book. It is convenient and useful to do so because they have similar ecological roles to play in the wildlife community.

2
VULTURES

Three species of New World vultures (family Cathartidae) now occur north of Mexico. The nearly extinct California Condor once ranged from coastal Washington southward to northern Baja California and, in prehistoric times, to Nevada, New Mexico, and Texas. Now it is confined largely to a remnant of its former range near Los Angeles. It is questionable how long the species will survive, as man's activities and pollution constantly threaten the few remaining condors. Nevertheless it is the responsibility of all concerned persons to try to assure the survival of this splendid Pleistocene relic.

The two remaining species, the Turkey Vulture and the Black Vulture, both are distributed widely in North, Central, and South America. The Turkey Vulture, in particular, has expanded its range northward during this century and seems to be continuing to do so. It has successfully reached southern Canada as a breeding bird. The northward expansion of the range of the Black Vulture is perhaps less dramatic, but these birds now nest successfully as far north as south central Pennsylvania. Stragglers occasionally even appear in southern Canada as non-breeding individuals.

The New World vultures are only superficially related to the Old World vultures, but both are classified as diurnal birds of prey in the order Falconiformes. Our vultures also are scavengers. The bulk of their food is fresh carrion, although Black Vultures occasionally are known to kill young pigs and other small, helpless

11

animals. On rare occasions Turkey Vultures also have been reported killing small animals. Neither species is well equipped to engage in such activity, however, because their legs and feet are relatively weak compared with other birds of prey such as hawks and eagles.

Each of our North American vultures is a large bird and a masterful creature in flight. The California Condor is the largest land bird in North America and one of the largest flying birds in the world.

Turkey Vulture

The Turkey Vulture *(Cathartes aura)* is the most familiar of the North American vultures. It occurs throughout all of the continent from southern Canada southward through Central America into much of South America. It is a large, dark brown bird. The naked head is crimson in adults. The wingspread is about six feet.

Turkey Vultures may nest in hollow logs, caves, rock shelters, among boulders on rock slides on mountain slopes, in foundations of abandoned buildings, or even under fallen logs and trees. They usually lay two eggs, but sometimes one or three are deposited. The eggs are attractive, largely creamy-white with brown, black, and other colors forming blotches. The incubation period is about 40 days.

On several occasions I investigated their nests in small caves or amid large boulders in mountainous areas. The nestlings retain their

Adult Turkey Vultures perching on cacti in the Southwest. Photo by M. Alan Jenkins.

An immature Turkey Vulture in flight.

white natal down for many weeks, and remain helpless during this period although they hiss, lower their heads, and often regurgitate the contents of their crops as an apparent defensive measure.

Awkward as Turkey Vultures are upon the ground, in flight these birds are masterful gliders and soarers. Along the Pennsylvania hawk ridges they soar effortlessly on updrafts for hours, scarcely finding it necessary to flap their wings. Similarly one commonly sees them flying over open, flat fields, as in southern New Jersey. Over the fields, the vultures are using thermals (rising bubbles of warm air) instead of updrafts to sustain their flight. Their habit of holding their wings in a slight V or dihedral helps observers to identify the birds at considerable distances.

Since the days of John James Audubon, controversy has raged over the method by which Turkey Vultures locate their food. Some naturalists argued that the birds use an extraordinary sense of smell in food-finding. Others insisted that keen vision is the answer. The dispute finally was resolved by Kenneth E. Stager who demonstrated experimentally that Turkey Vultures have both keen eyesight and a remarkably well developed sense of smell and that both senses are used in locating food, with olfaction (smell) playing a significant role. In its search for food, a Turkey Vulture generally flies low—barely skimming over ridge crests and trees—although when not looking for food it often flies it higher altitudes.

The Turkey Vulture's selection of food items also is somewhat different from that of other vultures. Carcasses of small animals form a considerable portion of their food although larger carcasses also are fed upon if available. Therefore Turkey Vultures occupy a feeding niche somewhat separate from the niche filled by Black Vultures.

Turkey Vultures from the northern part of their North American range sometimes engage in long distance north-south migrations, as a recent analysis of banding recoveries by Paul A. Stewart shows. For instance, one bird banded in Wisconsin was recovered about 2,063 miles south in Honduras. Other birds from the northern part of the range also traveled southward but only as far as the Gulf Coast states. In contrast, the birds living in the southern portion of the range in the United States tend to engage in much shorter migrations. However, some individuals from all areas do not migrate. Age apparently is not related to the migratory movements of these birds.

Although Turkey Vultures can live at least 16 years in the wild, most do not survive nearly that long. Indeed, the average annual mortality rate for the species in North America is about 21.5 percent.

Black Vulture

In comparison with the Turkey Vulture, the Black Vulture *(Coragyps atratus)* is a species of the southern United States although the extensive ranges of the two vultures overlap over much of Central and South America as well as the southern United States.

A Black Vulture is large and black with a short, square tail which extends slightly beyond the rear edge of the wings. Whitish patches on the undersides of the wings occur near the tip and are a good field mark. The birds fly with several rapid flaps followed by a short sail. This flight style is considerably different from that used by the Turkey Vulture and there generally is little difficulty in identifying the two species.

A Black Vulture in flight.

The nesting habits of this species are typically vulterine. No nest as such is constructed. Generally two eggs are deposited directly on the ground, sometimes on litter, in rock shelters, caves, hollow stumps, and similar more or less protected structures.

Of several Black Vulture nests shown to me during successive years by Theodore R. Hake, each was in a small cave on a hillside of a wooded ravine in southern Pennsylvania. Presumably the same parents selected the site each year although proof of this is lacking. In any event, these nesting efforts, along with an earlier reported nest near the historic Civil War battlefield at Gettysburg, Pennsylvania, are among the most northerly currently known for the species. 15

Nestling Black Vultures at a Pennsylvania nest site.

On my first visit to a Pennsylvania site, I was impressed at once by the color of the natal down of the young birds. Unlike the white down of nestling Turkey Vultures, the down covering the Black Vulture nestlings was pinkish-cinnamon. The nestlings retain much down on their bodies, even after the wing and tail quills are well developed. The birds also are considerably more aggressive than young Turkey Vultures of approximately the same age. They hiss, rush forward, attempt to bite a hand extended toward them, and sometimes revert to typical vulterine regurgitation in which the contents of their crop slowly are ejected orally.

In overlapping parts of the ranges of Turkey and Black Vultures, it is possible to study the ecological niches filled by the two species. As mentioned previously, Turkey Vultures often select small carcasses upon which to feed whereas Black Vultures congregate in large numbers at larger animals. Moreover, Black Vultures are fully capable of attacking and killing live animals such as young pigs, lambs, newborn calves, and even cows that are in a weakened condition.

Since Black Vultures lack the well developed olfactory sense of Turkey Vultures, they do not find their food by smell. However, some evidence suggests that Black Vultures generally fly at altitudes considerably higher than Turkey Vultures when searching for food and that, under some circumstances, they watch the lower flying Turkey Vultures and quickly gather at carcasses after the latter have located them. If a carcass is large, hordes of Black Vultures may drive a Turkey Vulture from the food. In the past, in southern cities, butchers had to watch their outdoor stalls carefully because Black Vultures eagerly eat fresh meat.

California Condor

The California Condor *(Gymnogyps californianus)* is the largest of the North American vultures and one of the largest birds in the world. It also is one of the rarest birds in the world. Current estimates indicate that only 40 or less still survive in a small remnant of their former range. New field studies conducted for the United States Fish and Wildlife Service by Sanford R. Wilbur show that there are two subpopulations which live in specific areas north of Los Angeles, California. Man's occupation of much of the breeding and feeding range required by the species, coupled with the unusually low condor reproductive rate, has played an important role in reducing the population to near extinction. Even today, illegal shooting, use of poisoned bait on grasslands near the condor refuge, drilling for oil along the edge of the Sespe Condor Sanctuary, and various other disturbances continue to threaten the survival of this magnificent species. Current plans to try to prevent the birds from becoming extinct are discussed on pages 157-159.

An adult California Condor. Photo by Fred Sibley/U.S. Fish and Wildlife Service.

Condors spend much of their time roosting and foraging. Their food consists entirely of carrion, particularly large carcasses such as cattle, calves, sheep, deer, horses, and ground squirrels. They apparently do not attack living animals. It is estimated that a California Condor requires about two pounds of food daily. Some efforts have been made to provide artificial feeding stations for the birds, and some concerned ranchers provide strict sanctuary for the birds when they visit the ranchers' lands at certain seasons of the year to feed, but all of these efforts have not halted a continual decline in condor numbers.

The future of the California Condor remains extremely precarious. Despite the world-wide attention devoted to this species, some people living near the current range of the big birds still resent them. One hunter threatened to shoot any condor he could find. Too easily, a natural or man-inflicted disaster could rapidly lead to the extinction of the species. Conservationists everywhere hope that final ending can be prevented.

King Vulture

At one time the King Vulture *(Sarcorhamphus papa)* occurred in Florida along the St. Johns River but this species no longer is found north of the Mexican border. It still lives in Central and South America.

3
KITES

Five species of kites occur in the warmer regions of North America north of the Mexican border. They are separated into five genera. The White-tailed Kite *(Elanus)* is of the same genus as other species which have a tropical or subtropical world-wide distribution. The Swallow-tailed Kite *(Elanoides)* is a tropical and subtropical New World bird. The Hook-billed Kite *(Chondrohierax)* is largely a bird of Central and South America. The Mississippi Kite *(Ictinia)* occurs from the central portion of the United States southward to Argentina. And the Snail Kite *(Rostrhamus)* is separated into three subspecies of which the race in Florida (known as the Everglade Kite) is almost extinct.

White-tailed Kite

The White-tailed Kite *(Elanus leucurus)* is a white bird with grayish wings and upperparts and black shoulders. The undersides of the wings and body are white, with a dark wrist patch. The tail is long and the wings are pointed.

This kite had declined drastically in numbers and, until recently, was in danger of extinction in the United States. However, it now appears to have reversed its declining population trend and is actually increasing in numbers in California. Eugene Eisenmann, who recently summarized the current status of this bird in North and Central America, reports that the kites have experienced a 19

remarkable population increase and breeding range expansion
since 1960. One recent California survey produced 626 White-tailed
Kites. Yet in 1935, John B. May wrote in *The Hawks of North
America* that the species was "in very real danger of complete
extirpation in the United States, where it is now very rare and local."

White-tailed Kites in California apparently have benefited
from current agricultural land use practices where they live in open,
cultivated bottomlands with scattered trees. The grassy slopes of
foothills containing oaks also are favored habitat types. An
additional requirement is an abundance of rodents upon which the
birds feed — particularly *Microtus* voles. The House Mouse *(Mus)*
also is an important food item.

Swallow-tailed Kite

The splendid Swallow-tailed Kite *(Elanoides forficatus)* is
fabled as one of the most delicate and graceful birds in North
America. Boldly contrasting dark and white plumage and deeply
forked tail make the birds unmistakable. Elliott Coues, one of the
great ornithologists America has produced, described the Swallow-
tailed Kite in Bent's *Life Histories of North American Birds of Prey:*

> Marked among its kind by no ordinary beauty of form and brilliancy
> of color, the Kite courses through the air with a grace and buoyancy
> it would be vain to rival. By a stroke of the thin-bladed wings and a
> lashing of the cleft tail, its flight is swayed to this or that side in a
> moment, or instantly arrested. Now it swoops with incredible
> swiftness, seizes without a pause, and bears its struggling captive
> aloft, feeding from its talons as it flies; now it mounts in airy circles
> till it is a speck in the blue ether and disappears. One cannot watch
> the flight of the Kite without comparing it with the thoroughbred
> racer.

North of Mexico the species currently is confined to southern
Florida although individuals occasionally wander far northward
from that subtropical region. My only experience with the bird in
the United States is a sighting north of the Everglades in March, but
in the mountains of Trinidad I photographed a number of these
birds swooping low over a mountain pass and was held spellbound
by their graceful beauty. I also observed these birds many times
along the lower Amazon in Brazil.

Swallow-tailed Kites build twig nests in the tops of tall pines or
other very tall living trees along trails or other thinly wooded areas.
Spanish moss is used as a lining for the nest. Two or three whitish
eggs usually are deposited.

The prey selected by the Swallow-tailed Kite is varied. Insects,
amphibians, reptiles, young birds, and the eggs of birds all appear
20 from time to time in its diet. Large flying insects are especially

important food items. John B. May also reported that a Swallow-
tailed Kite drinks while in flight, "like a huge swallow, by dipping
from the surface of quiet waters without checking its rapid course."

Hook-billed Kite

Within recent years a few Hook-billed Kites *(Chondrohierax uncinatus)* have been observed and photographed just north of the Mexican border in the Santa Ana National Wildlife Refuge in southern Texas. The species even has nested there successfully. These kites are among the species people most want to see on visits to the area.

Mississippi Kite

The southern and southwestern United States is the current range of the Mississippi Kite *(Ictinia mississippiensis)*. It formerly lived in some areas farther northward, but has retreated from those places. It is a falcon-like bird with long, pointed wings which are dark above and lighter below. The pale gray head and black tail are distinctive.

As a breeding bird the Mississippi Kite is attracted to small groves in Kansas, but in the southern states it occurs in heavily wooded areas where it nests in the forest canopy. The nest can be an old crow nest or one of its own from the previous year. Generally two bluish-white eggs are laid in a shallow cup lined with green leaves. Both sexes share in the incubation. The eggs hatch in about 30 to 32 days.

Mississippi Kites feed mainly, sometimes exclusively, on large flying insects. On rare occasions they also capture lizards and frogs. The birds are highly migratory, with a few specimens taken as far south as Paraguay and the Chaco of Argentina.

Snail Kite

Because of their endangered status, Snail Kites *(Rostrhamus sociabilis)* are well known to wildlife enthusiasts. Of the three good subspecies, only one occurs north of Mexico in the United States—*Rostrhamus sociabilis plumbeus*. It is confined to portions of Florida where it is known as the Everglade Kite. A few individuals of this same subspecies also occur in Cuba and the Isle of Pines. Other subspecies live in Central and South America.

Probably no more than about 70 birds still live in Florida. They are confined largely to the western edge of Lake Okeechobee and the southwestern section of Loxahatchee National Wildlife Refuge.

The breeding season for Snail Kites varies widely, but the normal period extends from late February until mid-June. The 21

An adult male Snail Kite at a nest in Florida. Photo by Allan D. Cruickshank.

birds tend to be fairly gregarious and normally nest in a loose colony. For example, five nests were used within a six- or seven-acre area in 1963 in Loxahatchee National Wildlife Refuge. The twig nests generally are placed eight feet or lower over water in shrubs and trees.

Snail Kites, like many forms of endangered wildlife, are rigidly dependent upon specific habitat and food requirements and appear unable to adapt to changing environmental conditions. In Florida the kites are restricted to specific freshwater marshes where they feed only on a freshwater marsh snail *(Pomacea paludosa).* Walter O. Stieglitz and Richard L. Thompson, who made a special study of the status of the Snail Kite for the United States Fish and Wildlife Service, report that the kites typically capture snails by flying slowly over a marsh at very low altitudes, casting back and forth, searching

An adult female Snail Kite in Florida. Photo by Helen G. Cruickshank.

for prey. "Spotting a snail," they wrote, "the kite drops swiftly and clutches the prey with its talons. Usually it carries the gastropod to a favored feeding perch where the snail is extracted from the shell and swallowed whole."

The future of the Snail Kite in Florida remains very precarious because the birds have suffered serious habitat destruction. In addition, careless hunters, other human disturbances, and possible pesticide pollution also seem to have negatively affected the birds. Some disease also may have occurred among the birds.

Despite these difficulties, the kites should be able to survive in small numbers if they continue to receive rigid protection and their essential habitat is protected and preserved. There is no doubt that the few remaining kites deserve such consideration as a unique part of the wildlife community of the United States.

4

ACCIPITERS

The genus *Accipiter,* containing the forest-loving hawks, is one of the largest of diurnal raptor genera. It contains 47 species. The genus as a whole is found world-wide although only three species occur in North America north of Mexico: the Northern Goshawk, Sharp-shinned Hawk, and Cooper's Hawk. The Sharp-shinned Hawk is the smallest of the three species and the most abundant.

Accipiters are characterized by their distinctive flight silhouettes—relatively short rounded wings and a long, rudder-like tail. The flight pattern also is distinctive and is an important clue to their identification. It consists first of several rapid wingbeats, then a short period of sailing flight, followed by more rapid wingbeats. Minor, but important, variations can be detected in the flight styles of each of the three species, aiding identification. Except during migration, when accipiters are seen most readily, they normally are confined almost entirely to forested or wooded areas and only rarely are detected unless one makes a special search for them.

These hawks are very high-strung birds and rely upon speed, agility, and suprise to capture small birds and mammals which form the bulk of their diet. They are important and effective predators in the areas in which they live. In the past they frequently were misunderstood and severely persecuted.

A female Northern Goshawk bringing a hemlock sprig to its nest. Photo by Heinz Meng. 25

The habitat in southern Vermont occupied by a pair of breeding Northern Goshawks.

Northern Goshawk

The Northern Goshawk *(Accipiter gentilis)* is the largest as well as the rarest of North American accipiters. As breeding birds in North America, these bold, powerful hawks are confined largely to Canada and the northern and northeastern United States. There is some evidence that the species is expanding its breeding range southward in the Northeast. The birds apparently are filling habitats and niches formerly occupied by Cooper's Hawks.

26

Nests which I studied in Vermont were located near small clearings or logging roads in mixed deciduous-coniferous forests. Frequently a plentiful supply of dead twigs and sticks littered the forest floor. The nest is formed of sticks and twigs and is lined with fresh evergreen sprigs or green leaves from deciduous trees. Three eggs commonly are deposited and incubated for about 36 to 38 days.

Northern Goshawks can be extremely fierce and aggressive toward intruders into their nest territories or at their nests. The ornithological literature contains many accounts of observers being attacked repeatedly, and sometimes injured, by these birds. However, not all Northern Goshawks exhibit such aggressive behavior. For example, at the nests I studied in Vermont the adults frequently landed on branches of birch trees about 20 to 30 feet from me and screamed their ringing *ca-ca-ca-ca-ca-ca* alarm notes. When I approached, the birds flew to new branches and, via this process, appeared to lead me up to one-half mile away from their nest. The

An immature Northern Goshawk migrating past a Pennsylvania hawk lookout.

birds then disappeared into the forest but reappeared again and repeated the performance upon my return to the vicinity of the nest sites. Only once, when I walked to a nest tree just after dawn one morning, did a Northern Goshawk dart toward me apparently in an aggressive effort to drive me from the nest. The hawk flew head-on toward me, repeatedly blending into the dim forest light so perfectly that, several times, she disappeared from view momentarily. Then, suddenly, she passed me and was gone in an instant. I was not struck but the experience was chilling. It gave me an insight into the terror which an animal must experience moments before being captured.

At irregular intervals, Northern Goshawks undertake spectacular southward invasions during autumn. The most recent of these occurred in 1972, when great numbers appeared throughout the northern and northeastern United States. Over 5,000 passed Duluth, Minnesota, and several hundred were counted passing the hawk lookouts at Bake Oven Knob and Hawk Mountain, Pennsylvania. Most of the birds were adults. This fact suggested that the hawks had reached a peak in their population cycle, that they experienced a poor breeding year, and that both factors were coupled with a widespread crash of the primary prey species throughout the northern breeding range. In 1973, an "echo flight" occurred but did not contain nearly so many birds as were seen the previous year, and in more recent years the numbers of migrating Northern Goshawks dropped to more normal levels.

Sharp-shinned Hawk

The smallest and most abundant of our three accipiters, the Sharp-shinned Hawk *(Accipiter striatus)*, occupies an extensive geographic range throughout North, Central, and South America. Leslie Brown and Dean Amadon recognize 10 subspecies of which only three occur north of Mexico. Of these the race *Accipiter striatus velox* covers nearly all of North America south of tree line.

These small bird-eating hawks typically select dense groves of conifers as nest sites in the northern part of their range. The nest is a stick and twig platform placed on a branch near the tree trunk, or in a crotch, fairly high above the ground. Four of five eggs usually are laid and incubated for about 34 or 35 days.

Sharp-shinned Hawks are important predators on songbirds in forested areas and therefore play important roles in the ecology of forest songbird populations. Only rarely do these hawks take prey such as insects and small reptiles and mammals. Apparently these bold hawks are somewhat selective also in respect to their choice of prey among birds. Some common forest songbirds seldom are

An adult Sharp-shinned Hawk in flight. Photo by Fred Tilly.

captured. Those birds which are taken are plucked before being eaten.

The best time to observe this species is during October, when large numbers are migrating southward along the Atlantic coast, the Appalachian ridges, and the northern shorelines of the Great Lakes. Some outstanding concentration points are Cape May Point, New Jersey, Bake Oven Knob and Hawk Mountain, Pennsylvania, Point Pelee, Ontario, and Duluth, Minnesota. At the two Pennsylvania sites, where the species is a common October migrant, one frequently observes Sharp-shins darting past the lookouts at close range. Sometimes they are readily lured toward artificial Great Horned Owl decoys, and are momentarily transfixed by the decoys. They are extremely high-strung; their wings and body quiver as they approach. Not infrequently they dive 29 and stoop at other passing hawks. Occasionally they capture migrating songbirds. Immature hawks appear first during migration, followed by the bulk of the adult Sharp-shinned Hawks later in October and early November.

Cooper's Hawk

Of the North American accipiters, the Cooper's Hawk *(Accipiter cooperii)* is intermediate in size between the two species previously discussed. It very closely resembles the smaller Sharp-shinned Hawk but generally is larger and the tip of its tail (when unspread) usually is very rounded.

Cooper's Hawks are far less common than the smaller Sharp-shinned Hawks—especially in the eastern United States. Indeed, there is increasing evidence that this species has declined seriously in numbers in the Northeast and that Northern Goshawks are beginning to replace Cooper's Hawks as nesting accipiters in southern New England forests and large wooded areas.

Despite these changes, Cooper's Hawks still occupy a sizeable breeding range extending as a wide band across the continent. They winter as far south as Central America with a few individuals occasionally reaching northern South America. They are not common breeding birds. Generally they are very shy and secretive about their nesting efforts. That was well illustrated in the late 1940's in central New York State when Heinz Meng located many more nests than previously had been known to occur in the area. He did this by carefully searching every likely wooded area or woodlot around Ithaca. Most of the hawks preferred mature beech, maple and hemlock, or oak-chestnut-hickory associations. But, in Massachusetts, white pine groves were preferred as nest sites. Meng noted that the nest trees usually were located close to the edge of a wooded area or clearing in the Ithaca area, and that large open fields frequently were nearby.

The stick and twig nest platform is placed in a crotch in the tree up to 60 feet above the ground. Shortly before the first egg is deposited, flakes of oak, maple, or hemlock bark are added to the lining of the nest. Fresh sprigs of hemlock or pine also are added. Generally four or five pale blue eggs are deposited. They are incubated for 36 days. Young males fledge when 30 days old, young females when 34 days old. However, the newly fledged hawks return to the nest to rest and feed.

The food habits of Cooper's Hawks frequently have been debated by game managers, hunters, and farmers who claim that these birds are serious predators on various game species and poultry. In point of fact, however, just the opposite is true. In a detailed and careful examination of the food brought to nestling

A female Cooper's Hawk bringing a chipmunk to her nest. Photo by Heinz Meng.   31

Cooper's Hawks in central New York, Meng discovered that
Common Flickers, American Robins, European Starlings, Eastern
Meadowlarks, and Common Grackles formed 87 percent of the
birds consumed. Starlings, in particular, were preyed upon heavily.
Of the mammalian diet of the hawks, Eastern Chipmunks and Red
Squirrels formed 94 percent of the species taken. Meng discovered
that birds formed 82 percent of the diet of nestling Cooper's Hawks,
and mammals 18 percent. Not a single chicken was captured by the
adult hawks although thousands ranged freely only 300 yards from
one of the hawk nests. Nor were any Ruffed Grouse captured. Only
four young pheasants were taken.

On the other hand, Cooper's Hawks sometimes visit bird
feeders during very cold periods in winter. At such times an
occasional songbird might be captured, but the hawks prey upon
such birds only to survive themselves. Such birds should not be
destroyed. Rather, they should be observed and enjoyed for the vital
force of nature that they are. If they must be removed, they should
be trapped alive and transported to a safe location some distance
from the feeding station.

5

SOARING HAWKS

The soaring hawks are the most commonly observed and abundant diurnal raptors in North America. They are represented by three genera—*Buteo, Parabuteo,* and *Buteogallus.* Of the three, buteos by far are the most common.

Red-tailed Hawk

Red-tailed Hawks (*Buteo jamaicensis*) are distributed over the entire continent south of tree line as well as on various islands in the West Indies and in much of Central America. They are extremely variable in color, even within a particular subspecies, and both pure albinos and melanistic birds are known. Black Red-tails seem to occur especially frequently in the West.

The Red-tailed Hawk is characterized by broad rounded wings, a fan-shaped tail when spread, and a relatively robust body. During migration, when soaring hawks ride updrafts along mountains and lake shorelines, they frequently take on a markedly different appearance. Then their primary flight feathers are folded, and their tails are not spread. This gives them a considerably more streamlined appearance.

Red-tails demonstrate a remarkably wide ecological tolerance for nesting and hunting sites throughout their extensive geographic range. A typical eastern bird may nest in a fairly mature wooded area or woodlot with little understory vegetation, adjacent to an old field or unused pasture where an abundance of rodents may be

34 An adult eastern Red-tailed Hawk showing its conspicuous belly band. Photo by Jan Sosik.

An immature Red-tailed Hawk circling over a hawk lookout in northwestern New Jersey.
Photo by Fred Tilly.

captured. In central New Jersey, for example, I noted a pair of Red-tails, present during several nesting seasons on an abandoned farm. The birds frequently hunted over several old fields surrounded on three sides by moderately mature second growth deciduous woodland in which the hawks probably nested. In southwestern Ohio, where G. Ronald Austing made extensive year-round observations on Red-tails, the birds usually preferred mature upland oak-hickory wooded tracts and woodlots and reached a breeding population density of about one pair per square mile. Some Red-tails, however, nested in less favorable lowland river 35 valleys that would seem more to the liking of Red-shouldered Hawks.

Elsewhere in the United States these birds live in various other types of habitats. In the Southwest, for instance, they nest on cacti in deserts. The species, therefore, shows an unusual ability to adapt to local environmental conditions.

Red-tailed Hawks are extremely important predators in the ecological systems they occupy. For example, in western Pennsylvania and eastern Ohio, where many old dead trees are allowed to stand in fields, one frequently observes Red-tails perched atop them and using them as hunting perches. But in the Pennsylvania German area of eastern Pennsylvania, where "clean farming" is carried out extensively and few dead trees and fencerows are allowed to remain, these hawks can be hard-pressed to find suitable hunting perches. I suspect that this lack of hunting perches may be an important limiting factor responsible for eliminating many Red-tails from areas which otherwise would be suitable for them.

The food habits of Red-tailed Hawks are extremely varied depending upon the age of the birds and where they live. Adult birds, for example, may capture *Microtus* voles and other rodents in large numbers, rabbits, an assortment of other smaller mammals, birds, snakes, and insects. Rattlesnakes sometimes are preyed upon in moderate numbers in the western portion of the range although the precise technique by which these venomous reptiles are captured is unknown. Immature Red-tailed Hawks tend to be much more restrictive in their selection of prey, at least in some areas. For example, in a study conducted by the Craighead brothers, immatures were limited more or less to small rodents, particularly to *Microtus* voles. Apparently as the birds mature their hunting skills become more effective and a wider selection of prey is taken.

In the eastern United States, notably along the Kittatinny Ridge in northwestern New Jersey and eastern Pennsylvania, Red-tailed Hawks are highly migratory during October and November. On cold days, with prevailing northwesterly winds, spectacular daily flights of these splendid hawks can be observed. The birds soar effortlessly on updrafts along the mountain and frequently pass observers at close range in a majestic procession in the autumn sky. At Hawk Mountain, Pennsylvania, Maurice Broun reported 1,144 Red-tails passing that spot on an October day in 1939. Single flights of that size have not been seen for several decades although Fred Tilly counted nearly 1,000 passing Raccoon Ridge, New Jersey, in early November 1971. However, during recent years larger Red-tail flights are now beginning to appear again along the Kittatinny Ridge. The ban on the use of DDT may be partly responsible for the increase in the number of birds. In addition, protective laws may also be helping to save some birds from being used as targets by hunters.

Red-shouldered Hawk

The Red-shouldered Hawk *(Buteo lineatus)* requires a habitat and ecological niche rather different from those of the Red-tailed Hawk. Red-shoulders are part of natural complex of five New World species that are referred to as woodland buteos. They also are among our loveliest and most vividly colored diurnal birds of prey. They have a discontinuous geographic distribution. One particularly colorful and isolated subspecies, sometimes referred to as the Red-bellied Hawk, is confined to a narrow strip of the West Coast in river valleys from southern Oregon (formerly) south to northern Baja California. The remaining four subspecies occur in eastern North America west to the plains and from the Florida Keys, southeastern Texas, and eastern Mexico northward to southern Canada.

Throughout their sizeable breeding range Red-shouldered Hawks generally select nest sites in river valleys or other areas with moist or swampy woodland. For example, considerable numbers of nesting Red-shouldered Hawks formerly lived in the extensive tracts of moist and/or swampy deciduous-coniferous woodlands on the Pocono Plateau of eastern Pennsylvania. Recent commercial and resort development in the area has reduced the breeding population of this species there, however, as has similar habitat destruction elsewhere throughout the Red-shoulder's range.

The stick and twig nest is placed at low to rather high elevations above the ground either in deciduous or coniferous trees. Occasionally abandoned hawk, crow, or squirrel nests are used as the foundation for a new nest and fresh materials are added to the old twigs and sticks. At the nests I studied in the Pocono Mountains of eastern Pennsylvania, mature beech, hemlock, and white pine trees were selected as nest sites by these hawks. One nest which I kept under periodic observation was placed about 35 feet above the ground in the crotch of a mature beech tree. The other nests, however, were all located higher amid branches of hemlock trees. The nests are easy to locate in suitable areas because tufts of down from the adults cling to the outer edges of the nests and provide an exceptionally useful clue to persons looking for new, active nests. Indeed, the technique is also useful in locating many other nests of raptors.

Generally three or four eggs are deposited at two- or three-day intervals. Fresh sprigs of hemlock or other leaves often are brought to the nest by the adults and used to cover the eggs. They hatch after about 28 days of incubation, and the nestlings remain in the nest for another five or six weeks before they fledge. The development of the plumage of the nestlings often shows a marked difference among them. At one of the Pocono Mountains nests, for example, one nestling was well developed at an age of about 21 days, but another nestling in the same nest still had much natal down present on its body. The behavior of the young hawks also varied considerably from bird to bird. One bird was extremely docile and easily handled, whereas one of its nest mates was extremely wild and aggressive. It was obvious that hawks have individual personalities.

The diet of Red-shouldered Hawks is typical of most other raptors in that a wide variety of food is captured depending upon season, location, and local ecological conditions. Among the more typical items consumed are small mammals and young birds, snakes, frogs, toads, and crayfish. Small mammals and several snakes were brought to the nest of the hawks I watched in the Poconos. *Sorex* shrews, which were plentiful on the forest floor in the vicinity of the nest, also have been taken by the hawks occasionally. Not infrequently Barred Owls, whose diet is similar to that of the Red-shouldered Hawk, occupy a similar feeding niche in much the same habitats selected by Red-shoulders. Because the owls are active at night, however, they don't usually compete with the hawks and the two species tolerate each other as members of the same wildlife community.

Broad-winged Hawk

Another of the woodland buteos, the Broad-winged Hawk *(Buteo platypterus),* is a small chunky species. It is a brown bird, lighter below, with two white and two dark tail bands. The continental subspecies occupies a large geographic breeding range extending eastward from the nonforested plains and southward from central Alberta and Nova Scotia to Texas, Florida, and the Gulf Coast.

The Broad-wing is a common nesting species in dry deciduous and mixed deciduous-coniferous forests. I studied nests in extensive forested tracts in southwestern Vermont, along the base of the Kittatinny Ridge in eastern Pennsylvania, and even on the forested slopes of the South Mountain range within the city limits of Allentown, Pennsylvania.

These hawks are relatively tame and sluggish birds. Sometimes they are seen perched beside old logging roads or other seldom used roads running through forested areas. Occasionally such birds can be approached closely, but at other times they fly across the roads and disappear into the forest. When they are discovered they

A Broad-winged Hawk soaring
on updrafts along a mountain.

sometimes give a whistle-like call similar to that of the Eastern Wood Pewee.

Broad-winged Hawks do not necessarily claim exclusive raptorial ownership of the forested areas in which they nest. One Broad-wing nest I discovered in a forest in Vermont was only about a mile from an active Northern Goshawk nest. The two species seemed not to interact or compete with each other, no doubt because they occupied different ecological niches in the forest.

Sometimes violent drama occurs at hawk nests. Such was the case at a Broad-wing nest located along the base of the Kittatinny Ridge a few miles from Hawk Mountain Sanctuary, Pennsylvania. The nest, containing two nestlings, was placed high in a large, mature white pine tree. When Alexander Nagy and I made our first visit to the nest the parents appeared overhead briefly but quickly disappeared. Upon climbing to the nest, I found two normal, healthy young hawks. But on another visit a week later we discovered only one living nestling. The other bird appeared to have died recently and was lying completely headless in the nest. Presumably it served as food for its surviving nestmate. The circumstances suggested a rare example of fratricide followed by cannibalism. Four other North American buteos also are known to engage in cannibalism on rare occasions. The following year this same nest platform was used by a pair of Great Horned Owls to rear their young.

Broad-winged Hawks are particularly well known to birders because of their spectacular mid-September migrations at various locations along the Appalachian ridges, the northern and/or western shorelines of the Great Lakes, and elsewhere. Thousands may be seen on peak flight days with hundreds of hawks in view at once as they "kettle" or flock within thermals and ride aloft in bubbles of warm air. Interested observers by the thousands come every year to concentration points such as Hawk Mountain, Pennsylvania, to witness these spectacular hawk flights. Many foreign visitors also arrive to enjoy what is one of the most dramatic animal migrations in the world. By early October, however, most of the Broad-wings are gone from the East, and other species such as Sharp-shinned Hawks replace them as the most abundantly observed species. These migrations are discussed later.

Swainson's Hawk

The western half of North America, from interior Alaska south to northern Mexico, is the summer breeding range of the Swainson's Hawk *(Buteo swainsoni)*. Although almost all

Swainson's Hawks winter on the pampas of Argentina, a few
hundred immatures winter in southern Florida every year.

In flight this species tends to hold its wings in a slightly uptilted
or dihedral position somewhat similar to that typical of Turkey
Vultures and Northern Harriers. During migration Swainson's
Hawks gather in very large flocks and make extensive use of
thermals in a manner similar to that of Broad-winged Hawks.
Swainson's Hawks may also take advantage of thermals to circle
high in the sky at other seasons of the year.

On the western prairies, where Swainson's Hawks are
common, they tend to be rather tame and sluggish raptors and
frequently prefer to perch on fence posts or other low objects rather
than hunt by circling overhead. Sometimes they even hop or hobble
about on the ground in pursuit of grasshoppers and other insects.
Locusts and grasshoppers are important components of their diets,
but bats and rodents, birds, reptiles, and amphibians also are taken.

During the breeding season, Swainson's Hawks build large
conspicuous nests of twigs, grasses, and other vegetation and place
the structures in relatively low trees or in giant cacti. Sometimes, in
forested areas, the nests may be up to 100 feet above the ground. At
other times low cliffs are used. A few nests also are placed directly
upon the ground. Two eggs are a typical clutch. After hatching, the
nestlings remain in the nest for about a month, then fledge.

During the spring and autumn migrations these hawks offer
impressive and extraordinary spectacles. As they funnel through
Central America, from or to their South American wintering
grounds, enormous flocks kettle in thermals, glide to new thermals,
and repeat the process again and again. Particularly large spring
flights have been seen by Central America's dean of ornithologists,
Alexander F. Skutch. Tens of thousands of hawks may be involved
in some of these flights which may require hours to pass across a
particular location. Sometimes Broad-winged Hawks and other
species join the flocks of Swainson's Hawks, adding to the
impressiveness of the flights. The migrations of this species are the
longest in distance covered of any North American hawk.

Zone-tailed Hawk

In contrast to the previous species, the Zone-tailed Hawk
(*Buteo albonotatus*) is not well known. By no means is it a common
raptor north of Mexico. Indeed, it barely crosses the Mexican-
United States border to breed in wooded canyons and along rivers
in the mountains of central Arizona, southwestern New Mexico,
and western Texas.

A Zone-tailed Hawk is largely black except for the tail which

41

contains three conspicuous grayish-white bands and a narrow grayish-white sub-terminal band. The forehead also is white. Immatures suggest the appearance of adults but have some white spots on the undersides of their bodies.

Zone-tailed Hawks have an unusual flight style. Most observers report that they are slow and sluggish, and that they mimic the flight style of Turkey Vultures in that they hold their wings in a V or dihedral much the same as Turkey Vultures do. The hawks are so skilled at this that observers must watch Turkey Vultures very carefully to be sure that they are not actually Zone-tailed Hawks.

The diet of these birds requires additional field study, but apparently consists largely of small fishes, lizards, and frogs. Small mammals and birds also are known to be taken occasionally.

Because this species is rare in the United States it is one of the birds which birders make special efforts to find on visits to the Southwest. However, the hawks should never be disturbed at their nests.

White-tailed Hawk

The White-tailed Hawk (*Buteo albicaudatus*) is equally as rare and little known north of Mexico as is the Zone-tailed Hawk. It lives on open grassy ranges and in chaparral country in southern Arizona and Texas southward through Central America into parts of South America where two other subspecies also occur. Adults are grayish with rufous shoulders and white on the undersides. The white tail has a bold black sub-terminal band.

As a breeding bird in Texas, this species is distributed locally along the coastal prairies from the Rio Grande delta to the upper coast, where large cacti, yucca, scrub oak, and other low plants are used to support the hawk's bulky stick nest. The birds use the same nest in successive years and merely add more material to the old structure. Two eggs usually are deposited. About two-thirds of them are white spotted with a few brown or lavender marks; the remaining one-third are white and unmarked. Not much is known about the incubation period or other details of the hawk's nest life.

Somewhat more information is available on the food habits of White-tailed Hawks. For example, in Texas they feed extensively upon rabbits although various other items including Cotton Rats, lizards, snakes, and frogs also are taken at times. A variety of insects such as grasshoppers, beetles, and cicadas also form part of the birds' diet. Birds are rarely captured.

Like the Zone-tailed Hawk, the White-tailed Hawk is among the raptor specialties of the Southwest. Birders particularly enjoy looking for this species and adding it to their life lists.

Short-tailed Hawk

The Short-tailed Hawk *(Buteo brachyurus)* is another South American species which barely reaches the southern borders of the United States. Current estimates put the Florida population at about 200 birds. They occur in both dark and light color phases, but in Florida most of the birds are in the dark phase.

The most detailed field study of the Short-tailed Hawk in Florida was made by John C. Ogden who discovered that the birds prefer mixed woodland-savannah habitats. Sometimes mangrove and cypress swamps adjacent to forest edge and open country are used as nest sites. The hawks are particularly adept at capturing adult birds of a variety of species, although some small mammals, reptiles, and amphibians also are taken.

Short-tailed Hawks capture prey by stooping in steep-angled dives from a "slow soaring" position or by stooping after first hanging motionless in mid-air. The hawks may stoop directly upon their prey, or may arrest their stoops with several motionless periods in mid-air. The prey is struck from above by the hawk's downward extended talons. At best, Short-tailed Hawks are only about 11 percent successful (efficient) in capturing prey. Studies on other birds of prey show that various other species also are roughly that efficient, too, but rarely more effective.

Current information suggests that Short-tailed Hawks engage in a migration entirely within Florida. From late February through early October the birds occur throughout the southern and central part of the state. A few individuals reach northern Florida. But from mid-October through early February almost all of the hawks nesting north of Lake Okeechobee apparently migrate to extreme southern mainland Florida. A considerable number of these birds winter in or near Everglades National Park. It is not at all unusual for sharp-eyed park visitors to see one or two of these birds if they carefully examine the hawks they see as they explore various trails and roads. Indeed, the sight of one of these birds is one of the special ornithological attractions of the Everglades.

Rough-legged Hawk

In contrast to the previous tropical and sub-tropical species, the Rough-legged Hawk is a holarctic species. It occupies an extensive Arctic and sub-Arctic belt across Asia, Europe, and North America. Of the four subspecies only *Buteo lagopus sanctijohannis* occurs to any extent in North America. Another race, however, barely reaches the outer Aleutian Islands.

Rough-legged Hawks are relatively large buteos and normally are observed south of Canada and Alaska only during late autumn, 43 winter, and early spring. Their plumage is extremely variable, and very complicated as one detailed study demonstrated. However, birders and ornithologists looking at these birds in the field generally recognize a light and a dark color phase. Additional details on age and sex recognition of this species are presented in *A Guide to Hawk Watching in North America* (Pennsylvania State University Press, 1979). Rough-legged Hawks are unusual among the hawks of North America because their legs are feathered to their toes. Only the Ferruginous Hawk and the Golden Eagle share this trait among our native raptors.

Rough-legs do not breed in the contiguous United States. Rather they breed on exposed cliffs and mountains with few trees, and on the wind-swept tundra regions of North America, Europe, and Asia. Their nests are constructed of sticks and twigs to which are added various Arctic plants, grasses, and mosses. Most nests are placed under overhangs on rocky cliffs, outcroppings, and ledges but occasionally nests also are put in the tallest of stunted trees on the tundra edge and along Arctic coasts.

Pairs of Rough-legged Hawks maintain several nests which are used year after year, sometimes alternately. Three or four eggs form the normal clutch. Because of the cold climate in which these hawks nest, incubation begins with the deposit of the first egg, to keep the eggs warm enough. Incubation lasts for about 28 to 31 days. By early July to mid-August the nestlings are about 41 days old and then leave the nest. The young hawks then remain in the Arctic for up to six additional weeks before migrating southward.

The food of the Rough-legged Hawks in the Arctic chiefly consists of small mammals such as lemmings. On Baffin Island in 1953, ornithologists George Miksch Sutton and David F. Parmelee noted that several nesting pairs of Rough-legs fed exclusively upon Collared and Brown Lemmings. On the hawks' winter range in the United States, however, *Microtus* voles are preyed upon heavily. Sometimes small rabbits also are taken; birds rarely are captured.

In eastern Pennsylvania during winter I noticed on several occasions that Rough-legs sometimes form loose hunting groups spaced across one-half mile or more of open field. Several hawks may be visible as they perch on trees along fence rows. Observers in other areas also have noticed similar groups from time to time. Some of these wintering birds are exceptionally tame and can be approached closely. Perhaps the hawks have had no previous experience with people and therefore show no particular alarm when they are approached. This makes the birds unusually vulnerable to illegal shooting and every year some of the hawks are shot by thoughtless hunters. This is unfortunate because this species

44 plays a very important role in the winter ecology of old fields and

other agricultural areas. Shooting the birds also deprives bird
watchers of the opportunity to observe and enjoy them.

Ferruginous Hawk

The Ferruginous Hawk *(Buteo regalis)* is a common species on
the Great Plains and is found also in the western United States and
the southern portions of western Canada. Arthur Cleveland Bent
points out that the specific name *regalis* is particularly appropriate
since it is a "splendid hawk, the largest, most powerful, and grandest
of our buteos, a truly regal bird. One who knows it in life cannot
help being impressed with its close relationship to the golden eagle,
which is not much more than a glorified *Buteo*. Both species have
feathered tarsi, both build huge nests on cliffs or trees, and both lay
eggs that are very similar except in size; the food habits, flight,
behavior, and voice of the two are much alike."

Although Ferruginous Hawks will occasionally place their
large stick nests on rocks or bluffs, nearly upon the ground, they
prefer tall trees whenever available. A hawk may line its nest with
roots, cow and horse dung, and even bleached bones. The hawks
have a tenacious attraction to their nests and use them year after
year, merely adding new material to the structures each season, until
they sometimes reach proportions of 12 to 15 feet in height.
Occasionally Great Horned Owls appropriate such nests, and not
infrequently magpies coexist with the hawks and nest amid the
sticks forming the base of the huge structure.

Unlike most large raptors which usually lay small clutches,
Ferruginous Hawks deposit from two to six eggs. Three or four are
typical. They incubate the eggs for about 28 days and the nestlings
fledge after about two months in the nest. The parents guard and
feed the fledglings for a considerable period until the young hawks
are capable of hunting successfully by themselves.

The literature on Ferruginous Hawks clearly demonstrates
that these birds feed extensively upon small to medium-sized
mammals. Ground squirrels and prairie dogs are preyed upon
heavily when available, but many other small rodents such as mice
and rats also are taken. Rabbits sometimes form an additional part
of the diet, and birds and snakes are captured on rare occasions.
When locusts and Jerusalem crickets swarm in vast numbers,
Ferruginous Hawks prey heavily upon them.

Roadside Hawk

The Roadside Hawk *(Buteo magnirostris)* is not normally part
of the North American raptor fauna. Indeed, it has been seen in the   45

United States only once—on April 2, 1901, in Cameron County, Texas. Normally the bird is a tropical species which can become very numerous in some places in Central and South America.

Gray Hawk

The Gray Hawk *(Buteo nitidus)*, or Mexican Goshawk as it was named formerly, is another of the buteos which barely crosses the Mexican border into the United States. However, small numbers occur in Arizona, New Mexico, and Texas where they nest in riverine forests. But, for the most part, the species occupies a geographic range extending through Central America to portions of Bolivia, Argentina, and Paraguay in South America. Nevertheless, in the extreme northern part of its range, as, for example, in Arizona, Arthur Cleveland Bent found the birds "quite common" in mesquite forest along the Santa Cruz River. They also occur in scattered groves, frequently in semi-arid regions. Now, however, the hawks are much less common than when Bent visited the Southwest. This is a small soaring hawk, gray above and deep gray below with fine barrings. Three conspicuous wide black bands cross the tail. The bird has a whitish rump.

Gray Hawks construct relatively small nests of sticks which frequently are concealed by leaves. The nests often are placed in trees in exposed sites and may range from 30 to 90 feet above the ground. They are lined with green twigs. Two eggs usually form the clutch; about 25 percent of all nests contain three eggs. The incubation period is unknown, but the young remain in the nest for about a month or a little longer. In Arizona, eggs are laid in May and the young fledge in early July. Farther south, however, Gray Hawks nest much earlier in the year.

Unlike most buteos which commonly feed extensively upon small rodents and other small mammals, Gray Hawks apparently prefer lizards and small snakes as their main source of food although beetles and large grasshoppers are consumed frequently. At times rodents and small birds also are captured and eaten.

Harris' Hawk

In contrast to the soaring hawks discussed previously, all of which belong to the genus *Buteo*, the striking Harris' Hawk *(Parabuteo unicinctus)* is sufficiently distinct from the buteos to be placed in the genus *Parabuteo*. As the name suggests, this genus has a close (although somewhat more primitive) evolutionary relationship with the genus *Buteo*.

Harris' Hawks are separated into three subspecies, two of
46 which occur in the southwestern United States from southeastern

An immature Harris' Hawk. Photo by Willis Peterson/U.S. Fish and Wildlife Service.

California and southwestern Arizona to southern Texas. The bird also extends its breeding range into southwestern Kansas. Thus the geographic range of the species extends from the southern United States southward to Chile.

The adult Harris' Hawk is blackish or sooty brown with bright chestnut shoulders, underwing linings, and thighs. There is a white terminal band on the tail and white upper and lower tail coverts.

In its limited range north of Mexico, the Harris' Hawk frequently is encountered in chaparral country where it often is seen on the ground or perched on low trees and bushes. In flight it soars in wide circles in typical buteo style.

Information is limited on the nesting activities of this species in the southwestern United States. The best studies are those conducted by William J. Mader in southern Arizona. Harris' Hawks in that area are nonmigratory and are strongly associated with saguaro-palo verde type habitats in flatlands of the Lower Sonoran Desert. The Harris' Hawks nest in adult pairs *and* groups of three—a most unusual situation. Oddly enough, the nests with trios of adults were 19 percent more successful than those with only two adult birds present. When trios existed, each adult had well defined roles to play in the nesting cycle. Sometimes all three birds cooperated in catching prey which generally consisted of about 57 percent mammals, 35 percent birds, and 7 percent lizards. Snakes were not taken although they were common in the nesting area. During winter the Harris' Hawks in southern Arizona tended to form groups of three to six birds which remained together for indefinite periods of time.

Common Black Hawk

The final soaring hawk considered here, the Common Black Hawk *(Buteogallus anthracinus)*, is a member of a group of three sub-tropical and tropical raptors. Leslie Brown and Dean Amadon recognize three subspecies of the Common Black Hawk. One lives in southern Florida, and the other barely extends its geographic range to the Southwest in summer.

This is a large hawk with completely black plumage except for one prominent white band and a narrow white terminal band crossing the tail. A small white area also is visible at the base of the primaries when the bird is in flight.

In the southwestern United States, Common Black Hawks inhabit forests and wooded streams which, in some cases, extend into hilly deserts. At times the hawks perch for long periods amid dense foliage in trees in heavily wooded areas.

Common Black Hawks nesting in the United States are known to place their stick nests in varied sites including the highest crotch of a tall mesquite remaining in a cutover mesquite forest rich in smaller bird life, in a cottonwood tree in a grove, in a fork of a

willow tree in a dense willow grove, or in other similar situations.
Nests range from 15 to 100 feet above the ground and sometimes are used for several successive years. Occasionally smaller birds such as flycatchers nest elsewhere in the same trees in which the hawks nest. In the northern portion of the species' range one or two eggs are deposited. Details are unavailable on the incubation period or on the length of time the nestlings remain in the nest.

Common Black Hawks feed upon a varied assortment of prey including insects, crustaceans, fish, amphibians, reptiles, and rodents. Birds rarely are captured.

Like several other raptors of the Southwest, this also is a species which birders look for and want to place on their life lists.

6
EAGLES

To see an eagle in flight is one of the most exciting and spectacular experiences in nature. In some parts of the world, as in Africa, where numerous species occur, eagles are incredibly abundant and easily seen. We are much less fortunate in North America. Here only four species of eagles occur: one a prairie and mountain form *(Aquila)* and the remaining three so-called sea eagles *(Haliaeetus)* because of their ecological affinities to coastal and other aquatic habitiats. However, two of these sea eagles are accidental stragglers to North America.

Golden Eagle

Despite the relative poverty of North America's eagle fauna, one of the species which occupies part of its geographic range here is the splendid Golden Eagle *(Aquila chrysaetos),* the King of Birds. Estimates of the number of Golden Eagles in North America place the population at anywhere between 8,000 and 50,000 individuals, but illegal shooting of birds wintering in the Southwest may have reduced that number seriously in recent years. The distribution of this regal bird, however, is by no means restricted entirely to North America. In fact, Golden Eagles are split into five subspecies and are holarctic; they occur as breeding birds throughout North America,

Eurasia, and North Africa.

Adult Golden Eagles are dark brown birds with golden-tipped feathers on the crown and nape. Immatures are more or less similar to adults but have much white on the base of the tail and on the wings. The amount of white varies with the age of the bird. Unlike the other North American eagles, these birds are feathered on the legs to the toes.

In North America Golden Eagles essentially are mountain birds at least as far as the breeding habitat is concerned. In the Northeast, where the remnant Appalachian population still survives, and probably does not number more than about 100 individuals, Walter R. Spofford reports that about a dozen active nest sites are known in New York, New England, and the Gaspé Peninsula of Quebec. Nests at these sites are almost always placed on cliffs, although one was constructed in a large mature white pine tree in the Adirondack Mountains of New York. In the Western United States, where the species is far more common, both cliff and tree sites are used. Not infrequently several alternative nest sites exist a few miles away from a nest in active use in a particular year and the birds sometimes rotate back and forth among nest sites at irregular intervals over a period of years.

The nest usually is a large, sometimes huge, stick and branch structure lined with sprigs of leaves from deciduous or coniferous trees. New material is added yearly. Two eggs form a typical clutch. In the colder, northern part of the Golden Eagle's breeding range, as in Alaska, eggs are laid in late May or June but, farther south in Canada and the United States, March is a more normal egg date, and, in the extreme southern fringe of the eagle's range in Mexico, the eggs are deposited in January or early February. The female does most of the incubating with occasional assistance from the male. The incubation period for most American Golden Eagles is about 35 lays, but elsewhere a period of 43 to 45 days is more typical.

According to Leslie Brown and Dean Amadon, the eaglets hatch at intervals over a period of a few days. In those nests in which two eggs hatch there is an 80 percent probability that the slightly older eaglet will kill its younger nest mate. Most nestlings fledge at an age of 65 to 70 days but continue to remain in the vicinity of the nest for another two weeks or so, then wander away from the site accompanied by their parents. Golden Eagles mature very slowly and do not become potential breeders until they are at least five years old.

Because these eagles are powerful predators, an enormous literature has developed regarding the food habits of the species in North America and elsewhere. The most comprehensive survey of the food habits of this species in North America was prepared by raptor biologist Richard R. Olendorff who examined 7,094 prey items taken by Golden Eagles. He discovered that mammals form 83.9 percent of the diet, birds 14.7 percent, reptiles 1.0 percent, and fish 0.4 percent. Hares, rabbits, ground squirrels, and prairie dogs were particularly important food items. Most field studies demonstrate that mammals, up to the size of deer fawns weighing roughly 15 pounds, form much of the diet of this eagle where mammals are plentiful. In addition to the mammalian prey already mentioned, a variety of other species also are taken, depending upon seasonal, geographic, and other circumstances. Some additional commonly captured prey include marmots, mice, rats, and voles. Even young of Mule Deer, White-tailed Deer, Pronghorn, Bison, and Bighorn Sheep occasionally appear in the diet of Golden Eagles. Birds also are taken from time to time. These may include Mallards, various hawks and owls, Blue Grouse, Sage Grouse, and Ring-necked Pheasants. In general, however, the eagles prefer mammals as prey when they can capture them.

In the western and southwestern sections of the United States, pointed differences of opinion exist between wildlife conservationists and sheep and goat ranchers (many of whom graze their livestock on public lands). The ranchers claim that Golden Eagles kill up to several hundred lambs and ewes each winter, thus resulting in an annual economic loss of thousands of dollars. This belief has led to wholesale and illegal aerial shooting of thousands of Golden Eagles in recent years in the Trans-Pecos and Edwards Plateau section of Texas, and parts of Wyoming, Colorado, and elsewhere. The magnitude and biological and ecological significance of this illegal eagle slaughter is discussed in a later chapter. Here, however, we can examine in somewhat more detail the role of eagles as predators upon sheep and goat livestock in the American West and Southwest.

The problem has received careful field study during recent years, particularly by qualified raptor biologists such as Walter R. Spofford who carried out several studies at the request of the National Audubon Society. Although there is little doubt that a few Golden Eagles wintering in the Southwest occasionally kill domestic lambs and ewes and thus cause some economic loss to ranchers, the magnitude and seriousness of the problem is almost always greatly exaggerated. Indeed, the problem is complicated by the fact that Golden Eagles readily feed upon carrion—particularly during cold weather. Not infrequently the carrion consumed takes the form of ewes and still-born lambs. Hence the mere sight of an eagle feeding upon a dead lamb or ewe does not necessarily mean that the bird killed the animal although ranchers usually jump to that conclusion. Many such lambs and ewes have proven to be stone

An adult Golden Eagle. Photo by Karl Maslowski/U.S. Fish and Wildlife Service.

cold upon critical examination, thus indicating that the eagles had not killed them. Indeed, only occasionally have such young animals been warm, the fact suggesting that the birds were responsible for making the kill.

The economic importance of raptors such as the Golden Eagle represents only part of the story. Throughout the extensive geographic range of this species, man has admired these regal birds for thousands of years. Today, in the United States, a more sophisticated attitude toward eagles, hawks, owls, and other predators is developing. Many people now are attempting to understand and appreciate the essential ecological roles which creatures such as Golden Eagles play in food chains and food webs. Even some ranchers now are willing to absorb a modest economic loss of some livestock in order to see and enjoy an eagle or other predator occasionally. In a very real sense the ecological and aesthetic values of birds such as the Golden Eagle cannot be overestimated.

Consider, for example, the special attractions offered by the few remaining Golden Eagles in the eastern United States, where these birds are extremely rare. Thousands of people often drive hundreds of miles to places such as Bake Oven Knob and Hawk Mountain, two famous hawk lookouts in Pennsylvania, to try to see one of the few dozen Golden Eagles which yearly migrate past these spots during October and November. It is impossible to place a monetary value upon such observations, but to these people the world is richer because eagles still appear in our skies. Over the years it has been my good fortune to have seen dozens of Golden Eagles from the lookouts at Bake Oven Knob and Hawk Mountain. The appearance of these majestic birds always is a highlight of the long hours and many days I spend studying hawk migrations on the eastern Pennsylvania hawk ridges.

White-tailed Eagle

In contrast to the Golden Eagle, sea eagles of the genus *Haliaeetus* mainly are associated with aquatic habitats—either coastal areas or inland lakes and rivers. They are large or very large, powerful, and spectacular birds and frequently have white tails or heads in the adult plumage. Such a bird is the White-tailed Eagle *(Haliaeetus albicilla)* which has been recorded along coastal Massachusetts once and in Alaska on rare occasions. Hence this eagle is included as part of the North American avifauna although it almost certainly will be seen here only on rare, isolated occasions. However, its extensive breeding range includes parts of Greenland and Iceland.

54

An adult Turkey Vulture.

An adult Saw-whet Owl.

A gray phase Screech Owl.

An adult Northern Goshawk.

An immature Golden Eagle.

Nestling ospreys.

A Barn Owl.

An adult Great Horned Owl.

An adult Bald Eagle in Utah. Photo by Fred Tilly.

Bald Eagle

Unlike the previous species, which has occurred on the North American continent only a few times, the Bald Eagle *(Haliaeetus leucocephalus)* occupies an extensive (but shrinking) geographic range in North America extending northward from Baja California and the southern tip of Florida to Newfoundland, southeastern Quebec, Manitoba, the Mackenzie River area, and northern Alaska. It is appropriate, therefore, that the species is the national bird of the United States of America.

An adult Bald Eagle is a spectacular and majestic bird. It has a gleaming white head and tail and a dark brown body along with bright yellow feet, legs, and bill. An immature, however, is dark brown with varying amounts of white on the wings and body depending upon the age of the individual. The species is divided into two subspecies one of which lives in Alaska and the other in the lower 48 states. The Alaska birds are larger and more abundant than those in the lower 48 states.

As would be expected of a member of the genus *Haliaeetus,* the Bald Eagle's prime feeding and nesting habitats are coastal areas as well as sites very near large inland lakes and rivers. In such places the birds engage in their seldom-seen courtship displays which are spectacular as two birds lock talons in midair, then plummet toward the ground in a series of somersaults.

55

Bald Eagle nests invariably are large stick structures. They may be placed in large trees or, less commonly, on rocky cliffs or directly upon the ground. In most cases they are in close proximity to water. Along the lower Susquehanna River in eastern Pennsylvania, where a sizeable breeding population of eagles once lived, many nests were built in mature trees on steep hillsides overlooking the river although the most famous nest in the region, the Mount Johnson Island nest, occupied a commanding view over an island and the adjacent river. Unfortunately eagles now are seriously reduced in numbers as breeding birds in this region and elsewhere in the lower 48 states, because of the effects of DDT pollution in the environment. However, in very recent years Bald Eagles in some areas have again raised young, and there is hope that this trend will continue now that some of the DDT and other harmful pesticides apparently are being eliminated from the environment.

In areas where these birds still occur and breed, they show a very strong attachment to traditional nest sites and characteristically add new materials to their nests every year, sometimes for as long as 40 years, until the structures become enormous—up to 12 feet high and 8 or more feet across—and weigh up to several tons. Some nests have become so large and heavy that they have broken their supporting trees and have crashed to the ground thus forcing the birds to construct new nests. The inner cup frequently is lined with pine needles or other soft material, and sprigs of green leaves frequently are added to the inner nest throughout the breeding season.

Two eggs generally are deposited. Egg laying dates vary considerably depending upon where in the breeding range of the species the birds are living. Southern Florida birds typically lay eggs during the period early November to late January whereas late March and early April are more typical months throughout much of the rest of the Bald Eagle's range. However, in the extreme northern portions of the range eggs may not be laid until early- to mid-May—after the lakes and rivers in which the eagles will fish have thawed. Curiously, for a species as widespread and spectacular as this is, the incubation period is known imperfectly. Many ornithologists state that 35 days is the normal incubation period but there are other published records ranging from 31 to 46 days. Females do most of the incubating although males sometimes assist for short periods.

The eaglets remain in the nest for about 10 to 11 weeks. Sometimes the smaller and weaker sibling is killed during this period. Like many raptors, the young birds spend much time flapping their wings in "practice flying" in preparation for departure from the nest.

An immature Bald Eagle.

Wintering Bald Eagles in Glacier National Park, Montana. Photo courtesy of Glacier National Park.

Because of their ecological affinity with aquatic ecosystems, Bald Eagles feed heavily upon marine and freshwater fish although birds and mammals occasionally also are taken. In many instances carrion, particularly fish, is consumed. For example, during the famous salmon runs on various rivers in southeastern Alaska, Bald Eagles feed heavily upon dead fish or upon parts of fish discarded by bears. At such times concentrations of between 3,000 and 4,000 eagles are reported in mid-November along the Chilkat River. At other times of the year, when live fish are captured, the birds swoop down upon the surface of the water and pluck the prey from the surface with their talons, then carry the prey to a suitable perch where the food is consumed. Occasionally they will even plunge into the water in an attempt to capture a fish. At other times a Bald Eagle will harass an Osprey carrying a fish and force the smaller bird to drop its prey. The eagle then swoops upon the falling fish, grasps it in midair in its talons, and claims it for itself.

The migratory behavior of Bald Eagles in eastern North America, particularly birds breeding in Florida, now is well known because of the extraordinary field studies of Charles Broley whose banding of large numbers of Florida eaglets eventually produced enough banding recoveries to demonstrate that these birds engage in a marked northward post-breeding dispersal. Thus most Bald Eagles seen migrating southward past such well known autumn hawk lookouts as Bake Oven Knob and Hawk Mountain, Pennsylvania, are Florida birds returning to their Florida nest sites. Prior to Broley's studies, the movements and migrations of these birds were poorly understood. During recent years the number of Bald Eagles seen as autumn migrants, particularly sub-adults and immatures, has declined sharply. This reflects the widespread reproductive failures of these birds because of the DDT-caused thin eggshell syndrome resulting in many eggs breaking during the incubation period (see chapter 15 for more details). In the future, however, if these birds are able to begin nesting successfully at more normal levels the ratio of adult to immature eagles passing the hawk lookouts in eastern Pennsylvania should swing more favorably toward the immatures again as it had always done before the massive use of DDT and other similar pesticides in the environment.

Steller's Sea Eagle

Steller's Sea Eagle *(Haliaeetus pelagicus)*, the final member of the genus recorded on the North American continent, was observed here only a few times in Alaska early in this century. The primary range of the species is along the sea coasts of Asia. This eagle is one of the largest and most spectacular birds in the world. It is a pity that these birds are not more widespread in North America. An adult is dark brown with striking areas of white on the forehead, wing coverts, tail, rump, and thighs. The tail is wedge-shaped. The bill, legs, and feet are bright yellow. Immatures are darker than adults and their white areas are rather dusky. The wingspread ranges from seven to eight feet. This eagle feeds largely upon fish although various birds, mammals, and other items including carrion also are consumed.

7
NORTHERN HARRIER, OSPREY, AND CARACARAS

The three living and one extinct species discussed in this chapter descend from widely divergent evolutionary backgrounds. They are not particularly closely related to one another aside from being diurnal birds of prey and being classified in the order Falconiformes. The Northern Harrier, for example, belongs to the genus *Circus*— a group of about ten species which, outside of North America, frequently are referred to as harriers. In North America, however, our single species often is called the Marsh Hawk. That all harriers are closely related is reflected in the fact that all the species, which show no particular evolutionary relationship with other genera, are placed in the distinct subfamily Circinae—one of a number of subfamilies within the large and diverse family Accipitridae.

The Osprey *(Pandion)*, too, is an extremely aberrant hawk which differs in so many respects from other diurnal raptors that it occupies its own distinct family, the Pandionidae. Finally the caracaras are more closely related to falcons than to other raptors 61 but they also are sufficiently distinct to warrant classification in a separate subfamily (Caracarinae) within the larger family Falconidae containing the true falcons.

Northern Harrier

The Northern Harrier *(Circus cyaneus)*, frequently called the Marsh Hawk in North America but Hen Harrier elsewhere in its extensive geographic range, is separated into two subspecies. *Circus cyaneus hudsonius* is the race found in North and Central America.

The adult male Northern Harrier is a strikingly attractive bird. It is largely ashy-gray, whiter below with rufous spots, and black wingtips. There also is a conspicuous white rump. Females are largely brown, and immatures brown with pale rufous or cinnamon on the undersides. Females and immatures also have the distinctive white rump patch.

Northern Harriers occur as breeding birds throughout Eurasia and extend their winter range into North Africa. North American harriers breed from Alaska, the Mackenzie River region, Manitoba, Ontario, Quebec, Labrador, and Newfoundland southward through much of the lower 48 states. They winter in Central America and on some of the islands of the West Indies. Occasionally a few individuals also reach northern South America during winter.

These birds have a much stronger ecological affinity with marshes, wetlands, and other aquatic habitats in North America than in Europe and Asia. Leslie Brown and Dean Amadon suggest that the lack of competition in the New World with other harriers with preferences for marshes and wetlands allows our birds to exploit an ecological niche in this part of the world rather freely. During the breeding season our harriers much prefer marshes rather than other habitats as nest sites, but in the Midwest they commonly are found in wet meadows and sloughs on the prairies and plains. Northern Harriers also are known to nest in swamps in New England.

The courtship flight of harriers is spectacular. In a series of nose dives, mainly performed by the male, the bird gracefully swoops to within 10 feet of the ground on fully extended wings from an altitude of about 60 feet (but occasionally as high as 500 feet). It makes from 25 to 71 U-shaped turns. At the top of each rise the hawk usually somersaults or turns sidewise—all in all an extraordinary performance.

The nest usually is built by the female and typically consists of dry straw, sticks, weed stems, and reeds with an inner lining of finer material including the tops of thistles, brake stems, and fine straw. 62 The eggs are laid at about two-day intervals. Five generally are

A female Northern Harrier carrying material to her nest. Photo by Allan D. Cruickshank.

typical but sometimes as few as four or as many as nine are deposited. They are incubated for about 24 days. Incubation begins with the deposit of the second to fourth egg, and is performed entirely by the female. The eggs are subject to a high mortality rate. In one North Dakota study, only 175 (58 percent) of the 303 eggs hatched. Similarly, harrier nestlings also suffer high mortality rates as demonstrated by a 71 percent loss in North Dakota and a 58 percent loss in New York State.

The physical development of the nestlings varies considerably because incubation begins before the clutch is completed. So, the eggs do not all hatch at the same time. The nestlings which survive 63 usually fledge in about 36 to 37 days—after they are fully feathered.

The hunting activities of harriers are a delight to watch, and no better description has been written than that of Arthur Cleveland Bent who recalled a picture of:

> Delightful days, now long past, when we sat for hours in a flimsy blind on the Cape Cod marshes, listening for the startling whistle of the yellowlegs or the mellow notes of the plover. The day is one of those lovely Indian summer days; only a gentle breeze is stiring, and the autumn haze softens the brilliant colors with which the waning summer has painted the marsh vegetation and the distant woods. As we sit there in the soft sunshine, dreamily drinking in the beauties of the scene, our eyes are alert to what is going on around us. Off on the distant mud flats are flocks of gray and white gulls, with scattered groups of shorebirds; over the extensive salt marshes black terns are winnowing the air, or plunging down into the grass for grasshoppers, and numerous swallows, now nearly ready to migrate, are skimming low over the meadows or the little pools; on a nearby sand flat some turnstones are digging holes in the sand; occasionally a great blue heron or a bittern flaps lazily over the marsh. There is always something moving; and, whether the yellowlegs and plover come to our decoys or not, we are sure to see, sooner or later, a dark speck in the distance that soon develops into a large, long-tailed, long-winged bird. On it comes with an easy gliding flight, its long wings slanting upward; as it turns we see its brownish breast and then its white rump, a young marsh hawk. A lazy, loafing, desultory flight it seems, but really it is full of purpose, as it quarters low over the ground in a systematic search for its prey. Often during the day it circles near us, but not too near, for all hawks have learned to avoid gunners. A peaceful day on the marshes would hardly be complete without an occasional glimpse of this industrious harrier, to add its touch of life to the picture.

Thus do these birds search for their food although, of course, they do not restrict their hunting efforts only to marshes. They also hunt for food in a wide variety of other habitats depending upon location, season, and circumstances. Therefore, the list of food items which are taken is long and varied. Small mammals, particularly *Microtus* voles, are very important prey items in many areas but rats, young rabbits and skunks, pocket gophers, squirrels, spermophiles (ground squirrels), shrews, and moles also are captured from time to time. In addition to the mammalian prey, a wide variety of birds as well as reptiles, amphibians, and insects also are taken.

During the autumn migrations, when harriers appear regularly in modest numbers along the Kittatinny Ridge in eastern Pennsylvania, sex and age classes of these birds exhibit rather markedly different migration patterns. Immatures, for example, appear early in the season in August and September, whereas adults of both sexes along with some immatures are seen during October. However, the adult males arrive in largest numbers late in the season, especially during November. Whenever the birds appear, they are welcome additions to the daily hawk counts and always a delight to observe.

Osprey

Anyone who has ever visited coastal New Jersey almost certainly has seen and been held spellbound by the sight of an Osprey *(Pandion haliaetus)* standing on its massive stick nest in a cedar tree or on a utility pole, or circling over expanses of salt meadows, or plunging into a channel or bay and rising with a fish clutched in its talons. Indeed, the Osprey is as much a part of the coastal scene as is the sea itself, or salt spray, or sand dunes. Of all of the birds of prey native to North America, to my mind none is more spectacular or more interesting than this splendid raptor. It is my favorite hawk and it shall be a very sad day for me, and a tragic loss of a priceless wildlife treasure, if Ospreys ever disappear from North America where they have become increasingly scarce during recent years.

A Northern Harrier quartering over a field. Photo by Jan Sosik.

Fortunately the Osprey is nearly worldwide in distribution, occuring (sparsely in some areas) on nearly all continents and large oceanic islands throughout the world. Hence it is unlikely that the species itself will become extinct although certain subspecies are seriously reduced in numbers. Even today, one can travel extensively over the globe and, in the correct habitat and during the proper season, be rewarded with the familiar sight of an Osprey fishing over some river or lake or perched in the top of a tall tree. During my own travels, I have seen these birds in the Caroni Swamp in Trinidad, deep in the interior of Amazonia, along the shoreline of Lake Albert in East Africa, as well as in many locations in North America.

Ospreys are just slightly smaller than eagles and are essentially brown above and white below. The white head of an Osprey is marked by a bold black patch running through the eyes and cheeks. They are, indeed, very handsome birds.

Perhaps the most interesting period in the Osprey's annual cycle is the nesting season after the birds have returned to their North American breeding grounds. Then one has unlimited opportunities to watch the birds regularly, or at will, and to become well acquainted with their habits and domestic activities. Throughout much of the breeding range of this species in North America, Ospreys return to their nest sites during late March or early April although geographic and weather conditions can alter this schedule considerably in some places. Males arrive first followed shortly thereafter by the females. It is stated frequently that pairs remain mated or pair-bonded for life, but if one is shot or otherwise disappears a new partner may be secured.

The Ospreys begin inspecting and repairing their old nest soon after returning. One bird, presumably the male, breaks dead twigs from trees with its feet, then carries the material to the female who arranges it in the nest. Early in the breeding cycle the birds sometimes engage in spectacular aerial displays as they soar, dive, circle, and chase one another in nuptial flight. At such times they also scream frequently and their loud, piercing voices can be heard from great distances.

Ospreys use a wide variety of supporting structures for their large stick nests. Along coastal New Jersey, nests frequently are built high in dead red cedar trees. Other structures also used include utility poles and lines, duck blinds, buildings, abandoned boats, large storage tanks, and wagon wheels attached to tall poles. Some New Jersey Ospreys also build their nests on low wood platforms placed on expanses of salt meadows for their benefit, and occasionally a nest is placed directly upon the ground. Elsewhere a wide variety of trees may be used as nest supports. Or the Ospreys may utilize as supports: steel towers for electric transmission lines, windmills, channel markers, fences and walls, stumps, or cliffs. Nests may be placed from ground level to 60 feet or higher above the ground. In some cases, they become enormous structures as a result of years of use, attaining heights of 10 feet and weights of many hundreds of pounds. Occasionally the trees holding the largest of these nests break and both nests and trees crash to the ground.

Ospreys develop very strong attachments to their nests. Some nests have been occupied yearly for about 45 years (perhaps by successive generations of birds?) although the normal period of use is much shorter. In some areas, as on Gardiners Island, New York, and Cedar Island, New Jersey, the birds breed in loose colonies sometimes containing dozens of pairs with nests occasionally as close as 60 or 70 yards apart. Elsewhere nests may be several miles apart.

Most Ospreys deposit three eggs in their nests, but occasionally two and rarely four are laid. They are fairly large and are boldly and richly blotched with various shades of browns and reddish browns which contrast vividly with the white, creamy-white, or pinkish-white ground color. Decades ago, when oology or egg collecting was a popular hobby in America, sets of Osprey eggs were considered among the most treasured additions to a person's collection and the birds suffered a terrible toll at the hands of nest robbers. Certain large collections contained hundreds of sets of Osprey eggs! Fortunately conservation laws now prohibit egg (and bird) collecting except for necessary scientific research and some educational purposes, the collecting done under authority of special permits.

The incubation period of North American Osprey eggs was given as 28 days in the older literature, but careful field studies by Peter L. Ames demonstrated that a period of 32 or 33 days is more accurate. The young, among the most handsome of our raptor nestlings, fledge when about 51 to 59 days old. Unlike most young hawks, they are very similar in appearance to the adults.

The food Ospreys eat is almost entirely fish—either saltwater or freshwater species including some of the more common types. An Osprey will hover, then plunge into a body of water with a huge splash, sometimes disappearing completely under the surface, then rise aloft carrying a fish clutched in its talons. The Osprey then carries the fish headfirst to the nest or to a nearby branch of a tree where it lands and eats. On extremely rare occasions other types of food, including birds, reptiles, and mammals, are captured. Such items form only minute portions of the diet of this fish-eating raptor.

Until about a decade ago, the Atlantic Coast between Virginia   67

An Osprey researcher examining the contents of a nest in New Jersey.

An adult Osprey with its young at a nest at Old Lyme, Connecticut. Photo by William C. Krantz/U.S. Fish and Wildlife Service.

and Rhode Island was world famous as a breeding ground for Ospreys. The bays, estuaries, and salt meadows of the region contained abundant nest sites and rich fish resources—two essential requirements for viable Osprey populations. But, even in this area of former abundance, a slow but continual decline in the population of breeding Ospreys has been in progress for many decades. The decline has accelerated during the past ten or fifteen years. Ospreys in this region and elsewhere in some parts of North America have experienced disastrous reproductive failures. Two areas offer typical examples: the population along the Connecticut shore in the vicinity of the mouth of the Connecticut River and the population along the southern New Jersey coastline.

According to Peter L. Ames, who made detailed field studies of the Connecticut River Ospreys, this colony once numbered about 75 nesting pairs and another famous colony of even larger proportions was located nearby on Gardiners Island in Block Island Sound. By the early 1960's, however, the Connecticut River birds began to fail to reproduce. Of 30 nests studied on or around Great Island, for example, only four eggs hatched and one bird fledged! Predators were thought to be partly responsible for some of the nest failures. Later studies demonstrated that pesticides, particularly DDT and related compounds, caused severe thinning of the shells of the eggs, so that eggs were broken during incubation. Today, slightly more than a decade later, this Connecticut River Osprey population is virtually extirpated insofar as breeding birds are concerned although within the past couple of years there has been some indication that the birds again may begin to nest successfully but in far fewer numbers than previously.

Similarly, Ospreys in southern Cape May County, New Jersey, also have become extirpated as breeding birds during the past 40 years. In 1937, Frederick C. Schmid examined nine locations in this area and found about 27 nests which produced 53 young. In 1938, about 21 nests produced about 45 young. And in 1939, 25 nests produced 56 young. A quarter century later, however, in 1963, these same nine locations contained about seven or eight nests which failed to produce a single young Osprey. Schmid suggested that combinations of factors probably were related to the extirpation of the Osprey as a breeding bird in southern Cape May County. For example, an enormous increase in the amount of human disturbance near Osprey nests, and actual displacement of the birds in some instances, contributed to their eventual fate. The use of large numbers of motorboats in bays and channels near occupied nests was particularly evident. Additionally, pound nets no longer are used in this area. These are shallow-water fish traps which, in the late 1930's, provided a readily available source of fish for Ospreys. Hence a gradually diminishing supply of fish also may have been an important contributing factor to the plight of this hawk. Finally, since World War II the serious pollution of the environment with DDT and related pesticides, as well as other industrial pollutants, also contributed to the reproductive failure of the Ospreys of southern Cape May County.

On the other hand, an important population of breeding Ospreys still survives in diminished numbers in the Seven Mile Beach area near Avalon in the northern section of Cape May County. Nearly a century ago, about 100 pairs of Ospreys populated Seven Mile Beach, but this extraordinarily high density was reduced to only 25 pairs within a six-year period after serious habitat destruction occurred in the wake of summer resort development, and perhaps other related environmental factors. In any event, 30 active nests still were in the area in 1927, and Joseph A. Jacobs found 29 active nests there in 1960. During the past decade, a further reduction in the Osprey population has occurred in this area.

In 1968, however, the State of New Jersey purchased 220 acres of Cedar Island near Avalon and set it aside as a wildlife sanctuary—one of the last strongholds of breeding Ospreys in New Jersey. When I visited this beautiful area with Joe Jacobs in 1965, many cherry, sassafrass, holly, and red cedar trees formed long lines along slightly elevated remnants of sand dunes and provided ideal

Osprey researcher Joseph A. Jacobs checking nestling Ospreys along coastal New Jersey.   71

Osprey nest sites. At the time of our visit in early July, most of the nestlings were well grown and large enough to be banded. They were splendid birds which strongly resembled the adults in the pattern of their plumage. As I photographed the birds being banded, some were docile but others were very aggressive. Even at this age, each nestling still retained its egg tooth on the tip of the bill—the calcium structure with which it broke free from the inside of the egg when it hatched. It would still be some time before the egg tooth gradually disappeared.

Despite the relatively good breeding success of the Cedar Island Ospreys, the productivity of this colony has been somewhat variable during recent years. The best information on these birds is provided by Joe Jacobs, who studied them for several decades. His records show that 18 active nests were on the island in 1966. Six of these successfully produced 11 young, all of which fledged. In 1970, 16 active nests were found, but in 1971 only four nests were used and only five young Ospreys were reared. By 1973, only one young Osprey was produced from 11 active Cedar Island nests. In recent years, however, the production of young has improved to some extent as DDT and other pesticides slowly are disappearing from the environment. In addition, certain Osprey management efforts seem to be helping the birds raise more young.

The serious population declines of some Atlantic coastal Osprey colonies are not peculiar to that area alone. In Michigan, Wisconsin, and Minnesota, the field studies of Sergej Postupalsky show similar population declines. However, within the past few years these birds also have been showing some welcome improvement in their breeding success.

On the other hand, various other North American Osprey populations are remaining at relatively stable levels, apparently because the ecosystems in which they live are not as seriously polluted with pesticides. Among the more notable stable populations are those in the Florida Bay area and some in the Chesapeake Bay area.

Ospreys are spectacular participants in the famous autumn migrations of hawks in eastern North America. At hawk lookouts such as Hawk Mountain on Pennsylvania's famous Kittatinny Ridge, bird watchers still can see in a single day several dozen migrating Ospreys during mid- to late September. The most extraordinary Osprey flight recorded along the ridge occurred one September day in 1965 at Bake Oven Knob, Pennsylvania, a few miles northeast of Hawk Mountain.

I shall long remember the day: cloudy, but with excellent visibility, moderately brisk northwest winds, and slightly cool air
temperatures. Throughout the day, an impressive movement of

Ospreys continued, but the highlight of the flight occurred during my last two hours on the lookout late in the afternoon. During that brief period, 40 Ospreys appeared! Once or twice, seven birds were aloft in a line approaching me in bomber-like formation. The mellow afternoon light cast the big birds in a soft reddish-pink hue, and long shadows from the mountain reached out and touched the adjacent valley. When the count finally was completed, shortly before sunset, an unprecedented total of 102 Ospreys had passed the Knob.

The Ospreys observed in autumn migrating past most of the hawk lookouts in eastern Canada and the United States winter from the West Indies southward into South America, whereas those birds from the Midwest winter in Panama, Colombia, and Ecuador. However, Ospreys from western North America (northern Idaho and eastern Washington) winter on the Pacific coasts of El Salvador, Honduras, and Costa Rica and thus do not overlap onto the wintering grounds used by Ospreys from the East and Midwest.

Crested Caracara

In contrast to harriers and Ospreys, especially the latter which are strong flyers, caracaras lack great flying style. Although they are more closely related to falcons than other birds of prey, they show none of the obvious qualities of grace and swiftness on the wing that one normally associates with falcons. Instead, caracaras are more vulture-like in their habits and more terrestrial than most birds of prey.

The only species still living in North America is the Crested Caracara *(Polyborus plancus)*. The distribution of this species is rather restricted in the United States. It occurs in central and southern Florida and in the Southwest. Crested Caracaras also occur in Central and South America, on the Isle of Pines off Cuba, and in the Falkland Islands.

The caracaras in Florida prefer open prairie regions. They are particularly common north of Lake Okeechobee on the Kissimmee Prairie. Typical habitat contains clumps of saw palmettos, some scrubby oaks, isolated cabbage palmettos, and some clumps of cypress. In Texas, where the birds now are rare, they prefer prairies and open pastures dotted with oaks.

As already mentioned, the behavior and food habits of the Crested Caracara are more vulture-like than falcon-like. Carrion and offal are readily consumed although live rodents and insects also are captured. In some areas caracaras have been reported to catch live fish and frogs. In southern Texas, W. C. Glazener watched caracaras rob vultures of their partly digested food by swooping low

An immature Crested Caracara on a Florida prairie. Photo by Allan D. Cruickshank.

over the feeding Turkey Vultures, forcing them into flight, then harassing them until they regurgitated their food. "Thereupon," wrote Glazener, "the pursuer flipped over into a dive and snatched one or more pieces of the falling food before it reached the ground. In three of the instances, the caracaras were observed to land and pick up additional material, presumably some particle missed in the aerial grab. All of the occurrences were out in open pastures where the view was not obstructed by trees or shrubs."

Unlike most birds of prey, Crested Caracaras spend considerable periods of time walking on the ground hunting for prey, and they also are fully capable of running rapidly. When they do fly, they sometimes suggest a Northern Harrier's flight pattern—an irregular or zigzag course, but with rapid wingbeats and long periods of sailing which give the birds a swift appearance.

The Crested Caracara is the national bird of Mexico where it is sometimes called the "Mexican Eagle."

Guadalupe Caracara

Before 1900 an insular species of caracara, the now extinct Guadalupe Caracara *(Polyborus lutosus),* lived on Guadalupe Island off the coast of Baja California. Discovered as late as 1875, this raptor was known to science for a mere quarter-century before being exterminated by man's ruthless acts. The story of its brief and tragic encounter with man is recounted vividly by James C. Greenway, Jr., in *Extinct and Vanishing Birds of the World.* It should serve as a severe warning of how fragile is the existence of many creatures with which we share the globe.

The last time the Guadalupe Caracara was seen alive was on December 1, 1900, when R. H. Beck visited the island and collected nine out of 11 individuals which, ironically, he thought to be abundant because of their tameness and his ease in finding them. We can hardly blame Beck for bringing the birds to the brink of extinction. In fact, goat herders purposefully shot and poisoned virtually all of the caracaras on the island because of their alleged predations on the young goats. The goats were introduced onto the island long before 1900. An estimated 40,000 or 50,000 animals lived there, where they caused enormous destruction to the native vegetation, at the time this endemic caracara became extinct.

Nor was the Guadalupe Caracara the only bird exterminated on the island from ravages of goats and men. Greenway reports that "39 percent of the breeding bird fauna of the island has been extirpated by the destruction of habitat and by introduced house cats which infest the island."

Similar stories, especially involving island faunas in many parts of the world, unfortunately are all too familiar to biologists and wildlife conservationists. They represent nature out of balance due to man's ignorance and rash, unnecessary actions.

8
FALCONS

The grace, speed, and agility of a falcon in flight, or diving at some unsuspecting prey, have inspired and captivated the imagination of man for centuries. Fortunately a fairly rich assortment of falcons occurs in North America. We have ample opportunity to see and appreciate these fine birds. Of the approximately 35 species of falcons distributed throughout the world, seven occur north of Mexico. All seven are true falcons and belong to the genus *Falco*. One of these is only an accidental visitor to our shores, however. And populations of several of our native falcons, especially the Peregrine Falcon, are seriously depleted because of widespread reproductive failures linked with DDT and other pesticide pollution of the environment and the contamination of the food chains of these predatory birds. Steps now are being taken to try to reverse the decline in numbers of these birds via a variety of management techniques which will be discussed later.

Gyrfalcon

The largest, and perhaps most prized, of all falcons is the magnificent Gyrfalcon (*Falco rusticolus*). It is an Arctic and sub-Arctic species which only rarely wanders south of the Canadian border into the lower 48 states. However, it is by no means confined to Alaska and Canada. Rather, it occupies an extensive range throughout the Arctic regions of North America, Europe, and Asia.

A Gyrfalcon. These are the largest falcons in North America.

It also occurs in Greenland and Iceland. It is the national bird of the latter country.

White color phase Gyrfalcons probably are the most handsome of all falcons. They are large, splendid, white birds marked on the backs and wings with gray-brown or gray spots and bars. Each has some streaking on the crown and some gray-brown barring on the tail. The feet, legs, and cere (membrane at base of upper part of beak) are bright yellow. Dark color phase birds occur as well in 77 various shades of slate gray or mottled white and gray. This species is exceptionally variable in its pattern of plumage coloration.

Gyrfalcons nest in far northern areas often beyond tree line. Typical of their habitats are barren tundra, mountains, and sea coasts. At times they also nest in Arctic woodlands. The birds do not nest every year. Nesting depends upon availability of the food supply at any given period.

Rather than constructing an actual nest as most other birds of prey do, the Gyrfalcon lays its eggs in a natural scrape or slight depression on a rocky ledge of a cliff often located in a gorge. Sometimes the falcon deposits its eggs in an abandoned nest of a Raven or a Rough-legged Hawk. An overhang usually extends over the nest or scrape, thus providing some protection from severe weather. An assortment of debris, particularly pellets and whitewash on a cliff face, is usually visible from far off.

From two to seven eggs are laid at approximately three-day intervals. In Alaska, four eggs form a typical clutch. They are creamy white and spotted and blotched with dark reddish-brown marks. The incubation period is reported at 28 to 29 days. The female does most of the incubation. The young falcons fledge when they are about 46 to 49 days old, but remain near the nest site for about a month while learning to hunt.

In the regions normally inhabited by Gyrfalcons, their food chains are short and relatively uncomplicated. Hence these large falcons are predators on a relatively limited number of prey species. The list is further reduced in number because falcons usually prefer birds as opposed to other types of prey. Thus, in coastal areas sea birds are readily taken along with duck and geese. Even small perching birds form part of the Gyrfalcon's diet in some areas. But in many parts of this falcon's extensive range ptarmigan and grouse represent the major portion of the prey items captured. In Alaska, for example, ptarmigan are reported to form 89 percent (by weight) of the diet of Gyrfalcons. In Norway 96 percent (by weight) of the diet consists of ptarmigan. Mammals, on the other hand, usually are represented only as a small percentage in the diet. Among mammals known to be taken are lemmings, hares, mink, and weasels.

Gyrfalcons rarely wander southward as far as the lower 48 states. At Hawk Mountain, Pennsylvania, where thousands of hawks are seen during migration each autumn, this species has been identified with certainty only three or four times since record keeping began in 1934. Nevertheless, every once in a while a Gyrfalcon appears somewhere in the lower United States, to the delight of birders and wildlife photographers. The most extraordinary recent series of sightings occurred during the winter of 1971-72 when about 59 individuals invaded the Pacific Northwest area, the Great Lakes region, and especially the Atlantic coastline from Newfoundland and Prince Edward Island southward at least to New Jersey. Two of these birds spent several months in Brigantine National Wildlife Refuge, New Jersey, and were observed, photographed, and enjoyed by countless people coming from far and near. Perhaps the abundance of potential prey in the refuge caused the birds to remain there since ducks formed at least part of their diet.

Prairie Falcon

In contrast to the previous species, the geographic range of the Prairie Falcon *(Falco mexicanus)* is in warmer regions of North America from southwestern Canada southward through the

A Prairie Falcon at a California eyrie. Photo by Ron Quigley.

western United States to Baja California. From an ecological point of view, the Prairie Falcon is more or less a counterpart of the Lanner Falcon of Europe. It normally is associated with plains or lower foothills which provide cliffs, bluffs, or canyons suitable as nest sites. During winter, however, as James E. Enderson found, Prairie Falcons in the central Rocky Mountain region "tend to concentrate in certain areas and are almost totally lacking elsewhere." Gently rolling farming areas with winter wheat are particularly attractive to the birds, apparently because Horned Larks occur there in large numbers and are important prey for the falcons. Indeed, at least in the Rocky Mountain region, the distribution and seasonal movements of Prairie Falcons and Horned Larks seem closely related.

By mid-March most Prairie Falcons have returned to their breeding range and are at their nest cliffs. If late snows force Horned Larks back to the plains (at least in the central Rocky Mountain region) the falcons leave the cliffs to follow their food supply. But, once settled at the nest sites, the males engage in splendid courtship displays—aerial dives, accompanied by loud screams, and strutting on the cliff ledges.

The nest sites generally are on perpendicular cliffs or rocky outcroppings from 30 to 400 feet in height. Some nests on cliffs in the Colorado River canyon were surrounded by towering canyon walls more than 1,500 feet high, making the nests virtually inaccessible to man. The nest itself, which is usually a scrape or depression on a ledge or a pothole in a cliff face, often is located at least 30 feet above the ground. In some areas lacking cliffs, Prairie Falcons nest in a variety of other sites, including dirt banks. Sometimes old abandoned hawk or owl nests on ledges are used. Often the nest faces south, but an overhang frequently extends over the nest ledge and provides some protection from sun and rain.

Four or five eggs usually are laid and incubated for 29 to 31 days mostly by the female. The nestlings are fairly well feathered when about 30 days old. They fledge about 10 days later. At least 80 percent of the birds do not survive through their first year.

According to Harold Webster, Jr., who made a careful study of Prairie Falcons in Colorado, these birds have much smaller appetites than Peregrine Falcons. They consume only about one-fourth to one-half as much food during the year as Peregrines do. Among the more important avian prey taken by Prairie Falcons are Western Meadowlarks, Mourning Doves, Horned Larks, Lark Buntings, Rock Doves, and even Burrowing Owls. Of the mammals forming part of the falcon's diet, the Thirteen-lined Ground Squirrel is a very important item. In Colorado, Prairie Falcons are reported to make an abrupt change in their diets, from rodents to birds, when the falcon eggs hatch. Even the swiftest of birds are not always immune from capture: Webster watched these falcons successfully catch in midair both White-throated Swifts and Violet-green Swallows. He also vividly described another spectacular example of the hunting effectiveness of a Prairie Falcon over a tall escarpment:

> As we approached this particular cliff, the old female falcon rose high into the air and screamed at us very indignantly for trespassing upon her domain. She soon towered high above us and, in a long downwind stoop, vanished from view. We were in a hurry to leave the vicinity lest we cause the brown-splotched eggs to become cold and hastened away from the cliff, leaving the eyrie in peace. About 75 feet south of the falcon's eyrie was a small pothole in the cliff containing the nest of an old Montana Great Horned Owl which had nested near her fast-flying neighbor for more than five years. We approached her nest very cautiously and, when all were in a position to watch her leave, we flushed the old owl off the nest. The old bird headed across a small open section to seek shelter in a grove of scrub oaks about 100 yards away, but when she reached the middle of the open area she seemed to explode in midair and drop lifeless to the ground. The old falcon had come up and dealt a lightning blow that immediately put an end to the career of the owl. The apparent ease with which the falcon had dispatched the owl urged us further to examine the bird which we found quite dead and torn open as if it had been given a tap with a sharp cleaver.

Most persons familiar with the Prairie Falcon state that the species has an unpredictable, excitable temperment. "One day a falcon is as calm as can be," wrote Webster, "and the next day, wilder than a hurricane."

Although the current population of the Prairie Falcon is known imperfectly, apparently the species is not in danger of becoming endangered. Nevertheless, it has declined in numbers in recent years. In some areas, however, such as the Snake River Birds of Prey Natural Area in Idaho, surveys show that Prairie Falcons are common breeding birds. A continuous program of monitoring population levels of this species is necessary to detect any serious population declines before the birds become too rare.

Peregrine Falcon

Unquestionably the Peregrine Falcon *(Falco peregrinus)* is the most famous, and perhaps swiftest, of all falcons. It is an extraordinarily spectacular species. Gerald H. Thayer described it well when he wrote that it

> is, perhaps, the most highly specialized and superlatively well-developed flying organism on our planet today, combining in a marvelous degree the highest powers of speed and aerial adroitness

An adult Peregrine Falcon. These birds once nested widely throughout North America but now are extirpated as breeding birds throughout much of their former range because of DDT pollution. Efforts are underway to try to reintroduce the species into its former haunts.

with massive, warlike strength. A powerful, wild, majestic, independent bird, living on the choicest of clean, carnal food, plucked fresh from the air or the surface of the waters, rearing its young in the nooks of dangerous mountain cliffs, claiming all the atmosphere as its domain, and fearing neither beast that walks nor bird that flies, it is the very embodiment of noble rapacity and lonely freedom. It has its legitimate and important place in the great scheme of things, and by its extinction, if that should ever come, the whole world would be improverished and dulled.

The Peregrine Falcon occupies an exceptionally large, indeed world-wide, geographic distribution with birds found (sometimes in limited numbers as nonbreeding individuals) on nearly all continents and on most large oceanic islands. Of the 19 subspecies recognized, three occur in North America as breeding birds and another subspecies accidentally reached our shores once or twice in the past. All three of the native subspecies currently are endangered.

When one thinks of Peregrine Falcons and the habitats they require, cliffs and mountain crags overlooking rivers come to mind immediately. In Pennsylvania, where this species once claimed occupancy of as many as 34 eyries, almost all were associated closely with cliffs along large river systems. Similarly, in New York and New England, where some of the most famous eyries in America were located, cliffs and mountain crags near rivers again characterized the Peregrine's selection of habitat.

Along one 55-mile stretch of the Hudson River, in the Palisades Interstate Park in New Jersey and New York, for example, nine eyries were occupied prior to 1961 on sheer rock walls. In the opinion of Richard and Kathleen Herbert, who studied these birds for over 30 years, four major factors were responsible for successful nesting there: (1) suitable nesting, feeding, and perching ledges, (2) an absence of large trees which impede flight and visibility, (3) the presence of long cliffs with several ledges rather than one narrow ledge, and (4) lack of disturbance from above at the nest ledges.

Along coastal areas such as Labrador, Ungava, and the Pacific Northwest, Peregrines frequently inhabit offshore islands where cliffs provide suitable undisturbed nest sites and an abundance of food from nearby colonies of nesting seabirds. On the other hand, occasionally Peregrines are known to nest in trees in Tennessee, and in various cities in North America they have nested successfully on ledges of tall buildings.

After a spectacular series of courtship displays in which the male, sometimes accompanied by the female, engages in superb aerial dives and undulations accompanied by much screaming, the breeding cycle advances to the egg laying stage. From three to seven eggs are laid either in a scrape or depression on the ledge of a cliff or directly upon the ledge. Typical clutches contain three or four eggs. The are absolutely splendid—perhaps the most striking and handsome of all bird eggs. The ground color ranges from creamy-white to pale pink over which are laid vivid small blotches or spots of rich reds and browns.

During the heyday of egg collecting, early in this century, Peregrine eggs were the most prized and sought-for of all oological treasures and the birds suffered unmercifully from the continual raids of egg collectors upon their eyries. Fortunately, Peregrine Falcons will lay a second and even a third set if the first is destroyed or disappears, but this imposes great stress on the birds. Falconers, too, raided the eyries early in this century and it seems miraculous that any young Peregrines were reared or fledged. In any event, the incubation period ranges from 33 to 35 days and both sexes regularly participate in incubation. The nestlings fledge at about 33 to 35 days of age.

The Peregrine Falcon is a superb, masterful hunter of birds. When it executes one of its spectacular stoops, which have made it world famous, it hurtles down upon some unsuspecting bird at speeds sometimes reaching 175 or 200 miles per hour and the prey instantly is dispatched in midair—sometimes in an explosion of feathers. Apparently the long hind claws cut the prey apart as if it were struck by a razor-sharp saber. Then the prey either falls to the ground or is held in the feet of the falcon and carried to a suitable place to be consumed. At other times Peregrines engage in long chases, repeatedly stooping at the intended prey, until it becomes exhausted and lands where it is either captured or escapes into available cover.

Peregrines are known to prey upon a long list of birds ranging in size from small wood warblers to ducks, small geese, and even hawks. In cities where Rock Doves are plentiful, these birds are taken readily by the falcons. In coastal areas, small seabirds form an important part of the Peregrine's diet. Both adults and young seabirds on the nest ledges are taken. On Little Tobago Island, West Indies, I once watched a Peregrine cruise back and forth along the top of a sheer cliff overlooking the open expanses of the Atlantic Ocean. Numerous gulls, terns, and tropicbirds nested on the ledges and slopes below and doubtless were preyed upon by the falcon. In areas rich in waterfowl, ducks of various species also are captured. Indeed, Peregrines sometimes are called Duck Hawks in North America.

During their southward migrations in autumn, Peregrine Falcons are far more abundant at coastal concentration points such as Cape May Point, New Jersey, than along the inland mountains of the Appalachians where soaring hawks such as buteos are seen in large numbers. But nowhere in North America today are these noble falcons now common. They have suffered massive reproductive failures caused by a combination of factors—especially pesticide contamination of food chains and altered reproductive chemistry related to the metabolites of pesticides which concentrate in the fatty tissues of the birds. Nevertheless, with a ban on the use of DDT and related compounds in the United States, there is hope that the species may still be able to recover to reasonably adequate population levels. Various captive breeding efforts and other management techniques also are aimed at that goal. This hope is not based upon wishful thinking. In Great Britain, where these pesticides have been banned from use, Peregrine Falcon populations (which also suffered from widespread pesticide-related nesting failures) have begun to breed successfully again. Presumably the birds will respond similarly in North America. Additional details on the various management techniques currently in use are discussed in a later chapter.

Aplomado Falcon

One of the Central and South American raptors which barely crosses the Mexican border into the Southwestern states is the Aplomado Falcon *(Falco femoralis)*. It is an attractive species with a bold face pattern and other distinctive markings. Relatively little is known about the species, especially in the United States, where it reaches the extreme northern limit of its range. Early in this century, the birds apparently were not overly uncommon in suitable locations, but now they are very rare north of Mexico. However, a few individuals still are seen occasionally on open plains covered with mesquite, cacti, and yucca. The birds apparently feed upon birds, mammals, lizards, and large insects.

Merlin

Although the Aplomado Falcon barely reaches the United States, the same cannot be said about the Merlin *(Falco columbarius)*. Indeed, Merlins not only are distributed widely as breeding birds in taiga, humid Pacific coastal forests, and prairie-parkland areas of North America, they actually occupy a panboreal distribution. The species is separated into several subspecies. In the most recent study of the systematics and evolution of North American Merlins, Stanley A. Temple recognized three subspecies. He speculated that the evolution of this falcon in North America involved two invasions from Asia during the Pleistocene. According to the theory, taiga and coastal Merlins evolved from the first Asian Merlin stock whereas prairie-parkland birds developed from the second Asian stock.

This species has not received much field study in North America. In northern Minnesota, where John and Frank Craighead studied the falcons on their nesting ground, typical habitat was described as

> a land of heavy timber interspersed with numerous lakes and bare, burned-over, open areas of glacier-scarred, metamorphic rocks. Spruce, birch, and tamarack grew in the low, swampy areas bordering the lakes. Jack pine, aspen, and birch occupied the higher ground and ridges, while the numerous islands were clothed with heavy, mixed strands of white pine, spruce, balsam, and a few old scattered jack pines. Bare rocks, large burned-over tracts, and numerous lakes formed the open areas; it was the type of country in which one would expect to find Sharp-shinned Hawks and Goshawks rather than falcons. Goshawks, Ruffed Grouse, and

Spruce Grouse were abundant in the heavy forest, while the Common Loon, the Goldeneye, and the American Merganser nested on the small islands in the lakes.

And in central Ontario, where Louise de Kiriline Lawrence studied these falcons nesting, mixed second growth forest near water, and with dead pine trees suitable as perches, was typical Merlin habitat.

The nest can be an old abandoned hawk, owl, or crow nest in a tree or a scrape amid dense vegetation directly upon the ground. Most nests range from 5 to 60 feet above the ground, 15 to 35 feet being most typical. From three to six eggs can be laid, but most clutches contain four or five. They closely resemble Peregrine Falcon eggs but are slightly darker. The incubation period is 28 to 32 days, with incubation beginning before the full clutch is completed. The nestlings fledge in about 25 to 30 days.

Merlins defend their nest territory vigorously against human intruders and other natural enemies such as hawks, crows, and large herons. However, small birds readily nest at will in close proximity to the falcon nests—sometimes even within the falcon's territory—without being molested by the raptors. In Ontario, for example, a variety of thrushes, vireos, wood warblers, and sparrows all nested without harm close to breeding Merlins. Apparently the falcons hunt at least one-quarter mile from their nests, particularly in open areas. Although Falconiform raptors all are diurnal, or active during daylight, these falcons occasionally are known to hunt at twilight. This crepuscular activity is quite unusual, however.

Despite the relative immunity from predation which songbirds breeding near Merlin nests enjoy, small birds nevertheless form a large proportion of the prey in the diet of this falcon. A wide variety of species are taken including such rapid fliers as swallows and swifts. Additionally, small mammals, insects, and occasionally other items also are captured. The falcons usually capture their prey with short, fast dashes and/or quick turns rather than the more spectacular stoops associated with larger falcons such as Peregrines.

Because this species breeds primarily in Canada, in areas seldom visited by most Americans, sightings of Merlins in the United States are of migrating birds during autumn or spring. In the eastern United States, Merlins appear in numbers during mid-October. Although a few are seen inland along the Appalachian ridges, most follow the Atlantic coastline southward. Concentration points such as Cape May Point, New Jersey, and Fire Island, New York, offer excellent possibilities for seeing these birds. Typical of falcons, Merlins cruise over the open salt meadows, sand dunes, and beaches rather than wooded areas which are more attractive to accipiters such as Sharp-shinned Hawks. The few birds that do appear inland along hawk ridges fly very low, just above treetops, which is an excellent clue to their identity. One must constantly remain alert or the birds can pass unseen because they fly very rapidly and usually are in view for only a few moments. Nevertheless, they add a good deal of charm to hawk watching on the ridges.

Kestrel

Within the genus *Falco* are a number of species which often are referred to as superspecies because they are very closely related to each other and apparently evolved from some common ancestor. Among the smaller falcons, the various species of kestrels provide a good example. These birds, of one species or another, are distributed widely in the Americas, Europe, Asia, Africa, and elsewhere. A typical example is a European species known simply as the Kestrel *(Falco tinnunculus)*. It is included in this book because it has occurred in the United States on two occasions. On 29 September 1887, a severely emaciated female was collected at Strawberry Hill near Nantasket, Massachusetts. Presumably the bird had flown across the Atlantic Ocean from Europe. Three-quarters of a century later another Kestrel, again an emaciated female, was found on 9 December 1959, in the West Indian village of Le Carbet on the west coast of Martinique. The latest American record for the species is an oiled bird trapped on 23 September 1972 at a banding station at Cape May Point, New Jersey. The species also has occurred once in Iceland and in Greenland. These birds, of course, are individuals which have wandered far outside of their normal geographic range. Their appearance in North America or the West Indies is purely fortuitous.

American Kestrel

On the other hand, the American Kestrel *(Falco sparverius),* the only kestrel native to North America, is distributed widely throughout the New World. The birds are the smallest diurnal raptors found in North America as well as the most colorful. They are the only small hawks in the continental United States and Canada with rufous-red tails. However, the sexes are dimorphic: males are considerably more colorful than females. The males have bluish-gray wings; females, brown wings. Other field marks also separate the two sexes.

American Kestrels exhibit examples of three types of protective coloration: countershading, disruptive coloration, and deflective coloration. The first is based upon the concept that animals are darkest where they receive the most light (the upper

88   A female American Kestrel. Photo by Harry Goldman.

surface) and lightest where they receive the most shadow (the lower surface). Thus, when an American Kestrel is viewed at a distance, its lesser markings on the underside are not discernible easily and the effect of relief is destroyed so that the bird is seen as a single plane. In contrast to this, the principle of disruptive coloration holds that perception of the true outline of an animal is hindered by the presence of conspicuous markings which do not resemble the real shape of the animal although they are clearly visible. In the case of the American Kestrel, the vertical black bars below the eyes are examples of disruptive coloration. Finally, deflective coloration is based upon the idea that conspicuous markings will misdirect an enemy's attack by creating a false representation of the prey's posture. Such markings usually suggest the presence of a head at the wrong end of the animal. Hence American Kestrels have markings which suggest a face at the rear of the head or on each side.

Open fields and agricultural areas are typical habitats for these birds although they also occur in towns and even in cities. Often, as one drives along rural roads, they are seen perched on fence posts, utility poles and wires, and in trees. After the birds have returned to their breeding areas in early spring, they wander over several square miles of terrain before actually selecting a nest site. They are fairly noisy during this period and often scream the *klee klee klee klee* calls from an overhead perch, or while flying back and forth from one spot to another. In eastern Pennsylvania, where I studied the biology and ecology of the species in detail, the selection of the nest site usually occurs during the first week in April, but it can occur as late as the end of May or even the beginning of June. Sometimes the male carries food to a prospective or symbolic nest box or cavity but this does not assure that that particular site will be the final choice.

In any event, the female joins the male shortly after he selects the nest site. She investigates it by entering and remaining inside for various periods of time. Many sorts of cavity-type sites can be selected, including holes and cavities in trees, bird boxes, buildings, and cliffs. These falcons also occasionally nest under the eaves of barns and other buildings, and even in unused chimneys. They are particularly attracted to suitable bird boxes and readily select them as nest sites, thus making construction and placement of the boxes and excellent conservation and wildlife management project. The birds do not gather nest construction material although debris from past nesting activities of other species sometimes remains in the nest sites being used by the falcons.

Four or five eggs form a typical clutch. They are laid on alternate days. Incubation begins before the full clutch is completed. In eastern Pennsylvania, where I marked American Kestrel eggs to determine incubation periods, incubation required from 28 to 35 days with an average of almost 31 days. In this area, the average sex ratio of nestlings was exactly half males and half females, but it varied considerably from year to year. The nestlings fledge when about 30 days old.

In the ecology of old field ecosystems, American Kestrels are important predators because they feed largely upon insects and *Microtus* voles although small birds also are taken when opportunities occur. Throughout the extensive geographic range of the species, however, a wide variety of prey is recorded as having been captured. Like all predators, these falcons are opportunistic to a great extent. They will catch whatever is most suitable, abundant, and readily available at any particular time or place.

Their hunting techniques vary. Frequently a bird will hover above a field, watch the ground intently, then drop upon an insect or vole. Among other North American falcons, hovering is very unusual. At other times, the birds dart out from a hunting perch such as the top of a tall, dead tree and capture the prey in midair. The food then is carried back to the perch where it is eaten.

During autumn, American Kestrels in eastern North America migrate mainly along the Atlantic coastline although some birds are seen inland at various locations. At times they occur in large numbers at various coastal concentration points. The most extraordinary flight on record was seen on 16 October 1970 at Cape May Point, New Jersey. According to Ernest A. Choate, who witnessed the flight, about 25,000 American Kestrels passed the Point that day! There is no adequate explanation for such an enormous flight, but it is likely that it represented the bulk of the American Kestrel population in eastern North America.

Once these small falcons arrive on their winter range, they establish winter feeding territories. Some field studies show that males tend to use habitats somewhat different from females, but additional studies are needed to define clearly the exact role of habitat separation among the sexes.

9

BARN OWLS

Owls are the winged hunters of the night. Unlike hawks, which are diurnal and relatively easily seen, most owls are entirely nocturnal and far more difficult to observe. Hence much less is know about them than is known about diurnal raptors.

All owls belong to the order Strigiformes. They are further divided into two families. One of these, the Tytonidae, contains the eleven species known as Barn Owls or, in some areas, Grass Owls. The various species of Barn Owls are distributed widely throughout the world although quite a few are insular and endemic in distribution. One species, however, known simply as the Barn Owl *(Tyto alba)*, occurs on most of the continents and larger oceanic islands of the world. In North America, where it occurs from extreme southern Canada southward, a single subspecies is recognized—*Tyto alba pratincola*. In various parts of the United States, the Barn Owl also is known as the Monkey-faced Owl, White Owl, and Golden Owl.

A Barn Owl is a delicately colored creature. It has a characteristic white, heart-shaped face, long legs, and feathered feet. The plumage usually is whitish below, often spotted with browns and blacks. The upperparts are buffy or rusty, the eyes brown.

Unlike most predators, which tend to avoid contact with man whenever possible, Barn Owls have associated fairly closely with man's activities and structures. For example, typical nest and/or

Barn Owls are important predators on rats and voles in agricultural areas. This young owl
92 was photgraphed in Oklahoma. Photo by Earl W. Craven/U.S. Fish and Wildlife Service.

roost sites often are located in old barns, towers of churches and schools, and water towers. Other sites include ledges of quarries, caves, hollow trees, and holes in banks. In the Chesapeake Bay area, many offshore duck hunting blinds are favorite nest sites. Moreover, these owls usually conduct their nocturnal hunting forays over old fields, pastures, and similar exposed areas where rodents are abundant.

Unlike most birds, which nest during the spring of the year, Barn Owls are known to breed during any season. Doubtless most nest during spring, however. In any event, a nest as such is not constructed. The five to eleven white eggs merely are laid directly upon the surface of the spot chosen to serve as the nest. Typical clutches contain from five to seven eggs. They are laid at two- or three-day intervals. Since incubation continues for 32 to 34 days, and begins shortly after the first egg is laid, the young hatch at different times. Hence they vary considerably in size and degree of development.

Nesting Barn Owls are fascinating creatures. In one nest in a dilapidated water tower near Gloucester, New Jersey, Julian K. Potter and John A. Gillespie were greeted by loud hissing noises as they attempted to locate the actual nest. Finally they found it in a hole in the floor of the structure. They wrote:

> Crowding back as far to the rear as possible, were five downy white objects, partly covered by an adult bird—undoubtedly the female. She had not budged from her duty, while the male had left when he suspected trouble. Evidently blinded by the flashlight, she stared with a most human expression. The nest cavity was approximately twenty inches deep, fifteen inches wide and eight inches high, the sides being formed by vertical floor beams, and the top and bottom by the floor and the ceiling of the room below. The stench of ammonia fumes issuing from this filthy hole was almost overpowering, and we wondered how any living being could exist in such an atmosphere. The hissing subsided somewhat when the flashlight was withdrawn. Was the adult bird making this noise or were the young ones responsible? The latter view, held by Potter, proved to be correct. The mother bird did not once make an audible protest. In size the young ones ranged from recently hatched to an advanced downy stage.

The voice of Barn Owls is particularly impressive and, when heard at close quarter, is long remembered. Potter and Gillespie describe it as "hair-raising" and "blood-curdling"—so much so, in fact, that it sent icy shivers up and down the spines of the two men! My own experiences with these birds fully confirm these impressions!

Despite the unfortunate and incorrect opinions which some people have about owls (and predators in general), the Barn Owl is an important predator in the habitats which it occupies. Much of its food consists of large quantities of rats and mice, particularly the prolific Meadow Vole *(Microtus pennsylvanicus),* although other animals, including shrews, birds, and insects also are captured occasionally. Sometimes these owls even stockpile quantities of voles at their nests—presumably for the benefit of the young which have not yet fledged. Barn Owls thus play significant roles in helping to control rodent populations. In turn, the owl populations seem to be tied to vole cycles. When the rodents are scarce, the owls also are scarce and vice versa.

The method used by Barn Owls to locate their prey, particularly under conditions of total darkness, remained a mystery until Roger S. Payne investigated the problem. It was already known that the ears of these birds are asymmetrical—one ear opening is located below and the other above the horizontal plane. These seemingly strange anatomical differences led to the discovery that, because of the differences, the owls can home in on the sounds made by movements of prey with the result that prey can be captured even in total darkness. Barn Owls are superb living mouse traps. Any farmer is fortunate to have these birds living on his property.

Barn Owls seem not to be particularly hardy birds, however. During periods of cold weather, or when snow is on the ground, many freeze to death or starve because they are unable to find rodents. Even predators are subject to factors which help to limit the size of their populations.

10

OTHER OWLS

Unlike the atypical Barn Owls which are placed in their own separate family, the remaining members of the order Strigiformes are placed in another family, the Strigidae. These are the birds referred to as the typical owls. In North America there are 17 such species separated into 10 different genera. They range in size from species as small as a man's hand to very large and powerful birds, and they are distributed from the Arctic to the sub-tropics, in a variety of habitats.

Members of the genus *Otus*, for example, are relatively small owls. The best known and most widely distributed representative north of Mexico, the Screech Owl, occurs from southern Alaska and Canada southward through the United States into Mexico. It is separated into no less than 18 subspecies.

Screech Owl

The Screech Owl *(Otus asio)* is one of the smallest of our owls with prominent ear-tufts. It occurs in two color phases, red and gray, regardless of age or sex. The eyes are bright yellow.

Throughout most of its range, the Screech Owl is a year-round resident. Some individuals in the northern parts of the range wander southward in winter, however. These owls occupy various habitats—forests, wooded canyons, orchards, and other areas with trees. Not infrequently they also occur in villages, towns, and even 95 in cities. Rivers, streams, or creeks frequently are an essential part of their habitat.

They may nest in various sites, particularly abandoned woodpecker holes and natural cavities in trees. Bird boxes intended for American Kestrels sometimes may be occupied by Screech Owls, and they have been found nesting in Wood Duck boxes. From three to eight white eggs can be laid, but four or five is the most common clutch size. The incubation period is estimated at 26 days. In at least one instance a pair of Screech Owls and a pair of American Kestrels nested together in the same nest; both species reared their young successfully. This was an interesting association since both raptors frequently share the same habitat and occupy similar ecological niches. However, the nocturnal behavior of the owls, and the diurnal behavior of the kestrels, prevent the birds from competing with each other directly.

Although small, this interesting and colorful owl is a vigorous defender of its nest. Indeed, of all the hawks and owls which I have studied and or photographed, including such powerful and aggressive species as Goshawks and Great Horned Owls, the only time that I have ever been struck by a raptor was while approaching a Screech Owl's nest. This aggressive behavior is well known. Arthur Cleveland Bent, for example, called the birds savage little brutes and considered them feathered wildcats—comparable to the "feathered tiger" reputation sometimes applied to Great Horned Owls. At one nest in a city near my home, Screech Owls defended their nestlings so vigorously—attacking anyone and anything coming close to them—that the local police shot the birds (illegally).

Before the advent of DDT and other organochlorine pesticides and their widespread use in orchards and other agricultural areas, Screech Owls were common nesting birds in orchards. They were vital ecological components of such areas because they captured large numbers of rodents, some birds, and insects. But few owls find enough food to support them in pesticide-drenched orchards now, and one is more likely to discover them living in wooded areas near running waterways.

This tendency to live near water is very strong in them. During one field study which I conducted, Screech Owls invariably responded vocally to a playback of a tape recording of a Screech Owl's voice whenever I was in the vicinity of creeks, streams, or rivers. Indeed, an occasional Screech Owl sometimes is found drowned in a Muskrat trap indicating that the bird was attracted to something in the vicinity of the trap—probably fish or amphibians.

The voice of the Screech Owl seldom is what its name suggests. Rather, its most typical sound is a quivering or tremulous whistle. The birds readily answer a whistled imitation after dark, and such

96

A red phase Screech Owl.

an imitation (or a tape recording of the sound) provides a good method of locating and censusing local Screech Owl populations.

As I have suggested already, the diet of this owl is extremely varied; a very long list of vertebrates, and some invertebrates, could be compiled based upon field studies conducted in various parts of the owl's extensive geographic range. Arthur Cleveland Bent stated the case well when he wrote:

> With such an extensive and varied bill of fare, it is difficult to arrive at any general conclusion as to the economic status of this owl. It depends largely on its environment and the most readily available food supply, for this owl evidently is satisfied with what animal food it can most easily obtain. Where mice, rats, and other small mammals are abundant, it apparently prefers them; in destroying them and in eating so many locusts, cutworms and other noxious insects, it is decidedly beneficial.

Placed in the context of an ecological framework, no species is detrimental or beneficial, however. Each animal has its place and function in the overall scheme of thing. Thus a Screech Owl, or a wolf, or a fox is important to the wildlife community of the area in which it lives.

Whiskered Owl

In the mountains of southeastern Arizona there is another small member of the genus *Otus* named the Whiskered Owl *(Otus trichopsis)*. Relatively little is known about this rather rare species. Although it is distinct from the Screech Owl, it resembles it even to the extent of occurring in red and gray color phases although gray individuals are more common than red. The most important characteristics which distinguish the Whiskered Owl from similar related species are the white spots on the scapulars (feathers arising from the shoulders) of the wings and the lower hindneck, large black spots on the underparts, and greatly developed bristly tips on the face feathers. Its voice also differs considerably from that of the Screech Owl, being a series of *boot-boot-boots* repeated rapidly. Its food apparently is restricted almost entirely to insects.

According to Joe Marshall (in Phillips' *The Birds of Arizona*), differences in habitat requirements in Arizona virtually separate the various *Otus* owls by altitude. The Flammulated Owl, which is discussed next, occurs in coniferous forests at higher elevations whereas the Whiskered Owl lives in dense woods of oaks and sycamores, or mixed oak-pine woods at middle altitudes. Screech Owls, on the other hand, occur in open woods in the foothills, valleys, and deserts. Other aspects of the biology of the Whiskered Owl probably are similar to those of the Screech Owl.

Flammulated Owl

The third North American representative of the genus *Otus* is the Flammulated Owl *(Otus flammeolus)* which occupies a geographic distribution more extensive then the Whiskered Owl, but nonetheless still is a western species. It occurs from southern British Columbia southward in montane areas west of the Great Plains to the highlands of Mexico and Guatemala. Its preferred habitat is the higher coniferous forests, particularly in areas where ponderosa pine abounds, or in open pine and fir forest.

Flammulated Owls are a little smaller than Screech Owls and, like the latter, also occur in gray and red color phases. However, the ear-tufts of Flammulated Owls are shorter than those of Screech Owls. The most important characteristic which distinguishes Flammulated Owls from closely related species is the color of their eyes—they are dark brown rather than bright yellow. The voice is a two-note *boot-boot*.

The three or four white or faint-creamy-white eggs are laid in an old woodpecker hole or natural tree cavity. The incubation period is unknown. Flammulated Owls feed almost entirely upon insects of various sorts although an occasional small mammal or bird also may be taken.

Great Horned Owl

When one thinks of large and powerful birds of prey, the Great Horned Owl *(Bubo virginianus)* certainly comes to mind. It is the largest "eared" owl native to North America, and it also is one of the most widespread, being distributed over almost all of the continent except in the extreme northern regions of the Arctic.

These owls are very variable in color. Individuals from the southeast, for example, are rather light whereas northwestern birds are quite dark. A typical Great Horned Owl is a very large and powerful bird with conspicuous ear-tufts. The upperparts are dark brown mottled with buff and white, whereas the underparts are lighter and finely barred with dark browns or black. The throat is white and the eyes are bright yellow.

Great Horned Owls frequently are thought of as occurring in remote wilderness and they do occur in such areas. However, they are equally at home in many other habitat types ranging from deserts, plains, and canyons to river bottomlands, scrub areas, and thickets. Arthur Cleveland Bent points out that Great Horned Owls and Red-tailed Hawks often are complementary species occurring in forested areas and in more open country. The owls are active as predators only at night whereas the hawks are diurnal in their behavior. My own experiences with these owls fully confirm this. I 99

A Great Horned Owl. These
birds are distributed widely in
North America.

found that some birds nested in mature forest in extensive woodland areas, others selected wooded hillsides overlooking reservoirs, and still others nested in exposed trees along creeks in otherwise open country.

As the annual avian nesting cycle starts, Great Horned Owls are among the first birds to begin. Their courtship, accompanied by much hooting, commences during January or early February. The birds do not build a nest of their own. Instead they use old squirrel, hawk, or crow nests. In Florida, Charles Broley even found these owls using Bald Eagle nests. But in many areas old Red-tailed Hawk nests are preferred. For example, G. Ronald Austing and John B. Holt, Jr., point out that this owl is more or less dependent upon Red-tails for nest sites in Ohio. The two species frequently alternate between several preferred nest areas; the owls use the nests built by the hawks the previous year. This causes the hawks to build new nests in an alternate location each year.

In addition to using old stick nests, Great Horned Owls occasionally use hollows in trees, broken snags, and similar sites as nests. On very rare occasions they even have been known to build their own nests. Sometimes these large owls breed in the same woodland for several years in succession but this apparently is unusual. Nonetheless, one nest which I studied in eastern Pennsylvania was used for two successive years after Broad-winged Hawks nested there the year before the owls claimed ownership of the site.

From one to five white eggs are laid, but two or three are more typical. The incubation period is estimated at 26 to 30 days but it may be longer. Because these owls begin their nesting cycle so early in the year, it is not unusual to discover the birds sitting on their nests, incubating their eggs, during snow storms. Sometimes they are covered completely with snow! During such periods of cold weather, careful incubation is essential to prevent the eggs from freezing.

The nestlings mature relatively slowly and remain in the nest for as long as 10 weeks before fledging. Shortly after hatching they are small down-covered creatures, but within three weeks they have grown remarkably. In one nest I visited regularly in eastern Pennsylvania, the nestlings at that age were covered with juvenal down and the feathers on their tails and wings were beginning to break through the protective sheaths. The birds still were helpless although they instinctively spread their wings as widely as possible, fluffed up their body feathers, snapped their bills, and made spectacular attempts to intimidate me and frighten me away from their nest. Presumably such defensive behavior works successfully in some instances.

The Great Horned Owl is a fierce hunter which occupies an ecological position at the top of the food chain. It is a necessary member of the wildlife community and should be enjoyed and protected as one of the most spectacular examples of our rich wildlife heritage. Although its diet is extremely varied, depending upon season and location, roughly one-half frequently consists of cottontails which accounts for its unpopularity among many hunters (who prefer to shoot them themselves). Yet the Great Horned Owl kills neither for sport nor for pleasure or recreation. It is an essential participant in the balance of nature of our forest ecosystems and, as such, removes surplus animals from the wildlife population. As a predator, it helps to assure that herbivorous mammals such as cottontails, which are capable of reaching enormous population levels if suitable conditions occur, do not increase to such large numbers that they vastly exceed the land's carrying capacity. Moreover, this magnificent owl also is a fitting symbol of the primitive American wilderness.

Sometimes it does not particularly smell so fitting, however. Not infrequently these owls prey upon skunks and, in the process, acquire rather unpleasant odors! Indeed, one cannot mistake a Great Horned Owl which has dined on skunk recently!

Despite the fact that horned owls are powerful predators, they have a variety of enemies. Unquestionably man is the most destructive. Countless thousands of owls have been shot by sportsmen in the past in the unrealistic hope that predator removal campaigns would create better hunting sport. They seldom, if ever, do. But, aside from man, horned owls have a variety of other enemies. It is well known, for example, that crows readily mob Great Horned Owls when they discover them roosting. Arthur Cleveland Bent described such encounters vividly:

> If an owl is discovered by a crow, the alarm is immediately given and all the crows within hearing respond to the call, gather about the owl, flying around or perching in the tree as near to the owl as they dare go, cawing loudly and making a great fuss. They seldom are bold enough to strike the owl, though I have seen them do so twice. The owl stands all this with dignified indifference, until his patience is exhausted, when he flies away with a string of crows trailing on behind; perhaps he has to move several times before he shakes off his tormentors or finds a secluded hiding place, where he can doze in peace. The owl seldom retaliates by striking one of the black rascals; in fact, I doubt if he ever does. But he gets even with them when they are in their roosts at night; I have heard of several crow roosts that were broked up by a great horned owl living in the vicinity; and many an owl has eaten crow.

Although these birds are permanent residents in the temperate parts of their range, owls living in the colder northern parts of the continent migrate southward when snows are deep and prey lacking. The birds return to their former range when environmental conditions become more acceptable to them.

Snowy Owl

In contrast to the Great Horned Owl, the Snowy Owl (*Nyctea scandiaca*) is well adapted to life in Arctic and sub-Arctic regions where it occupies a circumpolar distribution. The Snowy Owl is a very large white bird with a round head, but not a heart-shaped face. It is without ear-tufts, though George Miksch Sutton documents one bird with slight ear-tufts in a photograph published in *High Arctic*. Individuals are variable in color but many are flaked or barred (particularly females) with brown on heads and backs. The eyes are bright yellow.

In their Canadian and Alaskan breeding range, Snowy Owls are birds of the tundra where they sometimes occcur in large

Snowy Owls are Arctic birds that sometimes engage in southward invasions in winter. Photo by Leon C. Snyder/U.S. Fish and Wildlife Service.

numbers depending upon the abundance of lemmings, their chief food supply. However, during years of low lemming abundance, when the owls undertake their spectacular southward invasions into the United States, they usually occur in open fields, sandy beaches, barrier islands, and marshes—all areas which resemble tundra habitat.

On the tundra breeding grounds, the nest consists of a scrape or hollow on the gound on a mound or ridge. From three to thirteen white eggs can be laid, but six or seven form a typical clutch. The incubation, performed entirely by the female, requires 32 to 33 days. Near the head of Frobisher Bay in the southeastern part of Baffin Island, in the summer of 1953, George Miksch Sutton and David F. Parmelee found considerable numbers of Snowy Owls nesting. The birds defended their nests vigorously, flying low at the men when they approached within 100 yards of a nest or young. This particular abundance of owls apparently was due to few enemies (such as gulls and jaegers) in the vicinity, plus the availability of many lemmings.

Snowy Owl nestlings are sightless for the first four or five days after hatching, and it is not until they are 56 to 60 days old that they fledge. Under normal circumstances, the birds of the year remain in Arctic and sub-Arctic regions, but will join the adults in southward migrations when lemmings become scarce. These invasions are discussed in chapter 13. Briefly, they occur roughly every four years and correspond to lows in lemming population cycles. It is then that Americans sometimes have opportunities to observe and enjoy these beautiful birds. Often they are unusually tame, permitting one to approach closely before flying to another perch. In the past this lack of wariness frequently led to wholesale destruction of Snowy Owls, which were shot for "sport" and other frivolous reasons.

Not infrequently, during such invasions, the birds appear in cities and towns where they perch on television antennas, utility poles and wires, roofs of building, and cause a great deal of excitement since most people are unfamiliar with them. In rural areas, they sometimes remain in open fields which simulate tundra conditions. Here the owls usually find voles and other rodents which serve as satisfactory substitutes for lemmings. When rodents are in short supply, squirrels, rabbits, shrews, birds, and even carrion are consumed. Those owls which survive the winter return to the Arctic region in the spring.

Hawk Owl

The Hawk Owl *(Surnia ulula)* also is a circumpolar species, but it prefers the muskegs and coniferous forests of Alaska and Canada. The subspecies native to North America barely ventures south across the Canadian border during winter, and only rarely occurs well into the contiguous United States. It is a diurnal species, smaller than a crow, barred below with a long falcon-like tail. It frequently perches in an inclined position (not upright as do other owls) at the top of a tree, and jerks its tail. Its light face is framed by distinct black sideburn-like marks. The eyes are yellow. In flight it characteristically flies very low over the ground, gliding and flapping in a straight and swift manner. Sometimes Hawk Owls hover.

Nest sites can range from old stick nests of hawks and crows, to abandoned woodpecker holes in trees, to natural tree cavities. From three to nine white eggs are laid, five or six being typical. The incubation period is unknown. Food apparently consists chiefly of rodents and other small mammals along with an occasional bird or insect.

This interesting species, the most diurnal of our owls, occurs with some frequency along the northern borders of the United States in winter, but is an accidental visitor farther south. Hence it is an ornithological attraction when it appears well into the contiguous United States.

The vernacular name of the species reflects the fact that in appearance and habits it resembles small diurnal raptors. According to Arthur Cleveland Bent, the Hawk Owl's most striking feature is "its tameness, boldness, or utter lack of fear, perhaps largely due to its lack of familiarity with human beings. It has repeatedly shown no concern when closely approached and has even been captured by human hands."

Pygmy Owl

In contrast to the previous species, the Pygmy Owl *(Glaucidium gnoma)* is a western species ranging from southeastern Alaska southward through British Columbia to western Mexico and Guatemala. Its name reflects the fact that it is so small—not even equaling an American Robin in size. It is partly diurnal in its habits, is relatively tame, and is common in the deciduous and coniferous mountains of the West.

Pygmy Owls may live in more open coniferous or mixed forest, or in wooded canyons in arid areas. Typical nest sites are old woodpecker holes or natural cavities in trees. Three or four white eggs most typically are laid although as few as one and as many as eight have been recorded. The incubation period is unknown, but incubation apparently is performed entirely by the female. The nestlings are attended by both parents, and fledge at about four weeks of age.

The varied food habits of this owl include smaller species of mammals and birds along with reptiles, amphibians, and insects. Mice and larger insects probably are particularly important dietary items. Pygmy Owls are savage predators and frequently capture prey as large or larger than their own size. Some individuals prey heavily upon birds.

Ferruginous Owl

In wooded river bottoms and saguaro deserts near the Mexican border in southern Arizona and Texas another *Glaucidium* species, the Ferruginous Owl *(Glaucidium brasilianum)* reaches the northern limit of its extensive geographic range, which extends through all of Central America and South America. It is about the same size as the Pygmy Owl, which it closely resembles, but is somewhat more rusty in color. It also has streaks rather than spots on its head, its undersides are streaked with brown rather than black, and the tail is brownish with dark bars.

Ferruginous Owls rarely nest north of Mexico, but the few nests reported were abandoned woodpecker holes; such nests may be used year after year. Three of four, occasionally five, white eggs are laid. Although not particularly well known, the breeding biology of this species probably is similar to that of the Pygmy Owl.

Small to moderate-sized birds apparently form the bulk of the diet of the Ferruginous Owl. In Trindad, where I have observed or heard the species on several occasions, small birds of a wide variety of species respond rapidly and mob the owl at its whistle-like call (or at imitations of its voice). This suggests that it is a frequent predator on such birds. But in Tobago, where Ferruginous Owls do not occur, small birds of the species which responded on Trindad do not respond to an imitation of the Ferruginous Owl's voice.

Elf Owl

Although the previous two owls are very small species native to the southwest, there also is another tiny species which occurs in limited numbers in saguaro cactus deserts, scrub oak thickets, and wooded canyons in the arid southwest. It is the Elf Owl *(Micrathene whitneyi)* the smallest owl native to North America. The bird is only about five or six inches long.

Elf Owls usually nest in abandoned woodpecker holes. In deserts where the giant saguaro cactus occurs, they often use old flicker holes anywhere from 10 to 30 feet above the ground. In other areas, hollows in sycamore, cottonwood, or maguey trees are used. From two to five white eggs are laid, three being the typical clutch size. The incubation period is estimated at about 14 days and both parents apparently share in the incubation process. The age at which the young owls fledge is unknown.

The Elf Owl is such a diminutive creature that it hardly could be expected to prey upon very large animals, and food habit studies support this view. Its diet consists almost entirely of insects and insect larvae including crickets, grasshoppers, beetles, caterpillars, and centipedes. On very rare occasions it captures small birds.

Unlike the Pygmy and Ferruginous Owls, which are more or less diurnal in their habits, the tiny Elf Owl is decidedly nocturnal and usually remains hidden in a hole in a tree or amid a dense thicket of foliage during the day. The birds become very active at twilight, however, and sometimes fly around campfires—perhaps because they are attracted to insects (which themselves are attracted by the light).

Burrowing Owl

The Burrowing Owl *(Speotyto cunicularia)* is another of the fascinating raptors of the western United States, southwestern Canada, and Florida. These birds frequently live in burrows in prairie dog colonies. In the past, thousands of these owls were reported living in some colonies. But as the mammal communities were reduced in size due to man's activities, or have disappeared entirely, the owls also have become scarce in some areas. In addition to using prairie dog burrows, the owls also use deserted burrows of other mammals such as woodchucks and skunks.

In addition to the birds in the western United States, another subspecies of the Burrowing Owl occurs in central and southern Florida. These birds frequently inhabit prairies and airports, where suitable habitat occurs. During recent years the breeding range of the Burrowing Owl in Florida has been expanding northward. The owls are using extensive open areas with grazed or mowed grass, and fences suitable for perches. Hence the birds apparently are taking advantage of changes inflicted upon the land by man, particularly those caused by an expansion of the cattle industry in northern Florida. These Florida birds excavate their own burrows.

Major Charles Bendire, an Army officer and ornithologist serving in the West about a century ago, made particular note of the habits of birds of prey, including the nesting habits of the Burrowing Owl. He wrote in Bent's *Life Histories of North American Birds of Prey:*

> When not disturbed, the same burrow is used from year to year; in such a case it is cleaned out and repaired, if necessary. In different localities their choice in the selection of nesting sites varies somewhat. At Fort Lapwai, Idaho, they generally selected a burrow

on a hillside with a southerly exposure, while at Walla Walla their nests were always found in burrows on level ground. At Camp Harney, Oregon, where the Burrowing Owls were not very common, one under a large basaltic bowlder [sic] seemed to be a favorite site with them, and here they encroached upon the timber in the foothills of the Blue Mountains. At Fort Custer, Montana, I found them mostly on level ground, generally bottom lands, and always at the outskirts of a prairie dog village. On the Pacific coast the burrows of the ground squirrel are more often used for nesting sites, and occasionally those of badgers, which are quite common in some sections. If one of the former is selected, it has first to be considerably enlarged, and which [sic] requires a good deal of patient labor on the part of the Owls to accomplish. While stationed at Fort Lapwai I had an opportunity to see an Owl at work enlarging and cleaning out a burrow. The loosened dirt was thrown out backward with vigorous kicks of the feet, the bird backing gradually toward the entrance and moving the dirt outward in this manner as it advanced. These burrows vary greatly in length and depth, and are rarely less than 5 feet in length and frequently 10 feet and over. If on level ground they usually enter diagonally downward for 2 or 3 feet, sometimes nearly perpendicularly for that distance, when the burrow turns abruptly, the nesting chamber being always placed above the lowest part of the burrow. If in a hillside it will frequently run straight in for a few feet, and then make a sharp turn direct to the nesting chamber. At other times the burrow follows the curves of a horseshoe, and I have more than once found the eggs in such a burrow lying within 2 feet of the entrance and close to the surface of the hill on a trifle higher level; where, had it been known they could have been reached with little trouble. These burrows are generally about 5 inches in diameter, and the nesting chamber is usually from 1 foot to 18 inches wide. After the burrow is suitably enlarged, especially at the end, dry horse and cow dung is brought to the entrance of it, where it is broken up in small pieces, carried in and spread out in the nesting chamber which is usually lined with this material to a thickness of 1 or 2 inches, and I have never found any other material in the nest. In California, however, they are said to line them occasionally with dry grasses, weed stalks, feathers, and similar materials. On one thing most observers agree, namely that their burrows invariably swarm with fleas.

Burrowing Owls lay from six to eleven white eggs, but most typical clutches contain from seven to nine. The incubation period is estimated at about three weeks, and both parents participate in the incubation process. The age at which nestlings fledge is unknown.

Although Burrowing Owls are known to feed upon a considerable variety of prey, insects and rodents form the bulk of their food. Among the more common insects which are captured are locusts, grasshoppers, Jerusalem crickets, mole crickets, black crickets, dragonflies, caterpillars, and so forth. The owls' mammalian diet includes various rats and mice, ground squirrels, young prairie dogs, and a variety of other species.

A Burrowing Owl in Loxahatchee National Wildlife Refuge, Florida. Photo by W. H. Julian/U.S. Fish and Wildlife Service.

The behavior of Burrowing Owls in a colony is described beautifully by Elliott Coues in Bent's *Life Histories of North American Birds of Prey*:

As commonly observed, perched on one of the innumerable little eminences that mark a dog-town, amid their curious surroundings, they present a spectacle not easily forgotten. Their figure is peculiar, with their long legs and short tail; the element of the grotesque is never wanting; it is hard to say whether they look most ludicrous as they stand stiffly erect and motionless, or when they suddenly turn tail to duck into the hole, or when engaged in their various antics. Bolt upright, on what may be imagined their rostrum, they gaze about with a bland and self-satisfied, but earnest air, as if about to address an audience upon a subject of great pith and moment. They suddenly bow low, with profound gravity, and rising as abruptly, they begin to twitch their face and roll their eyes about in the most mysterious manner, gesticulating wildly, every now and then bending forward till the breast almost touches the ground, to propound the argument with more telling effect. Then they face about to address the rear, that all may alike feel the force of their logic; they draw themselves up to their fullest height, outwardly calm and self-contained, pausing in the discourse to note its effect upon the audience, and collect their wits for the next rhetorical flourish. And no distant likeness between these frothy orators and others is found in the celerity with which they subside and seek their holes on the slightest intimation of danger.

The enemies of the Burrowing Owl are relatively few. Man's destruction of prairie dog towns takes a heavy toll of these owls, by the use of poisons and by the sealing of burrows. Also, rattlesnakes enter some burrows used by owls. The reptiles are seeking rodents, or shelter, but they nonetheless prey upon some owl eggs and young. Otherwise this fascinating owl seldom is threatened by enemies.

Barred Owl

Among the large to very large North American owls are species of the genus *Strix*. Three such species occur north of Mexico. Of these, the Barred Owl *(Strix varia)* occupies the largest geographic range. It occurs from southern Canada southward over the continent, and westward to the Rockies. Throughout this range, it frequently is associated closely with Red-shouldered Hawks, both species commonly preferring wet or swampy forests. Sometimes, however, Barred Owls live in relatively dry woodlands.

Barred Owls are large, grayish-brown, "earless" owls. The white underparts have crosswise barring on the breast and lengthwise streakings on the belly—features which are characteristic field marks.

The nest sites preferred by the Barred Owl are abandoned hawk or crow nests or cavities in trees. No nesting material is taken into

110

natural cavities, but the owls sometimes add fresh sprigs of green vegetation to hawk or crow nests when they are selected as nest sites.

From two to four white eggs are laid, two being most typical. The incubation period is estimated at 21 to 28 days, but the former almost certainly is incorrect. The female is said to do most of the incubating.

The Barred Owl is one of the more common and interesting members of the wildlife community. In the South, it is the typical hoot owl of swamps and wet woodlands. Its hoots are not as deep as those of the Great Horned Owl, but they are more emphatic. They generally occur in a series of eight—two groups of four. Roger Tory Peterson describes the sound as *"hoohoo-hoohoo . . . hoohoo-hoohooaw"* and states that the *"aw"* closing the second series drops off in a particularly characteristic manner. When heard from a distance, the Barred Owl's hooting resembles a dog's barking. Some observers have even nicknamed these birds "eight hooters" because of their distinctive vocalizations.

Barred Owls feed upon a wide variety of prey: mammals (particularly rodents), birds, reptiles, amphibians, fishes, and insects. Even small owls are captured occasionally, demonstrating that predators also are preyed upon. Some of the owl's hunting is done in broad daylight. According to Arthur Cleveland Bent,

> Barred owls, as well as some other large owls and hawks, have well-marked feeding nests, old nests to which they carry their prey to tear it up and devour it at their leisure. Such nests are often well decorated with downy feathers, and I have been tempted to climb to them on several occasions. One of these . . . contained the posterior half of a large hornpout (fish), the hind leg of a cottontail rabbit, numerous bits of fur and feathers, and about a handful of small, white fish bones, such as are found in kingbirds' nests. These feeding nests are generally not far from the breeding nests, in the same patch of woods.

Spotted Owl

Taking the place of the Barred Owl in the western United States is another member of the genus *Strix*, the rare Spotted Owl *(Strix occidentalis)*. Its geographic distribution is restricted to a narrow strip of the Pacific Coast from southwestern British Columbia southward through California, and eastward through the southern Rocky Mountains from central Colorado southward through eastern Arizona, New Mexico, and western Texas into parts of Mexico.

In appearance, Spotted Owls resemble Barred Owls but they can be distinguished from their eastern counterparts by the horizontal barrings of their underparts.

Preferred habitat seems to be forested canyons, mixed woodlands, and dense coniferous forests. Spotted Owls apparently do not occur where Great Horned Owls live; if horned owls move into an area, Spotted Owls leave. Relatively little is known about this rare species, but, judging from the available information, Spotted Owls select natural cavities in cliffs, floors of caves, and cavities in trees as their nest sites. Only rarely do they occupy abandoned nests of other birds. From two to four white eggs can be laid, but most clutches contain two. The incubation period is unknown, nor do we know at what age the nestlings fledge.

The food of the Spotted Owl consists largely of small mammals such as wood rats *(Neotoma)* and other common rodents. At times, bats also are captured, and Spotted Owls are known to feed on Pygmy Owls on occasion. Bent states that the Spotted Owl is decidedly nocturnal in its habits and usually sleeps during the day in a shady retreat. He also states that it is a very tame (or stupid) owl, with an extremely gentle nature.

Great Gray Owl

The Great Gray Owl *(Strix nebulosa)* is the third North American representative of the genus *Strix*. It is the largest owl (24 to 33 inches) found on the continent, although much of its size is accounted for by its extraordinarily fluffy plumage. Its body actually is only slightly larger than that of the Barred Owl. A Great Gray Owl is a dusky-gray bird with a round head without ear-tufts, unusually large facial discs, a black spot on the chin, and heavy lengthwise striping on the underparts. It has an unusually long tail (12 inches). It has yellow eyes.

This splendid bird is distributed throughout much of the western half of Canada and Alaska, with a southward extension of its range in the Sierra Nevada and Rockies. Its preferred habitat is dense coniferous forest in Canada and Alaska, but in the southern part of its range it lives in mixed woodlands bordering such coniferous forests.

It selects abandoned hawk nests placed high in conifers, or (rarely) hawk nests on rocky walls, as its own nest site. Two or three dull white eggs form a typical clutch, although as many as five have been found. The incubation period is unknown. In fact, relatively little is known about this owl because of the remote areas in which it lives. However, like many owls from far northern areas, Great Gray Owls are unusually tame (probably because they seldom, if ever, have contact with man). They are reported easily approached—if one is fortunate enough to find a bird.

From what is known about the diet of the Great Gray Owl, its food consists largely of small mammals such as hares, young rabbits, and various other smaller species including squirrels, rats, mice, and shrews. Apparently small birds also are captured occasionally. Much remains to be learned about all aspects of the life history and ecology of the Great Gray Owl.

Long-eared Owl

The Long-eared Owl *(Asio otus)* is distributed widely throughout parts of Europe, Asia, and North Africa as well as throughout most of the contiguous United States and southern Canada, during one season or another. Excluded from its geographic range are the far northern regions of Canada, the far western and northwestern parts of that country, and Alaska. The bird also does not occur in Florida and the Gulf coast region of the United States. Long-eared Owls are separated into several subspecies, two of which occur in North America.

These owls are approximately crow-size. They are relatively slender birds which, because of their long ear-tufts, sometimes are confused with the considerably larger and more robust Great Horned Owl. They are brownish birds, darker on their upperparts, with lengthwise streaking contrasting with the lighter underparts. The ear-tufts are closer together than on the other species of tufted owls. The eyes are yellow.

Long-eared Owls have a variety of habitats. Both coniferous and deciduous forests and woodlots are used, usually in close proximity to fields or other open areas. The owls commonly are observed sitting motionless on a limb against the trunk of a pine tree or other conifer. Sometimes a number of owls gather in communal roosts during winter in the North.

Although Long-eared Owls have been recorded nesting on the ground on rare occasions, most nests are in abandoned hawk, owl, crow, or squirrel nests. Several nests which I studied in eastern Pennsylvania were stick and twig structures placed about 20 to 30 feet above the ground in a dense pine woodlot. The birds usually roosted in this same woodlot during winter.

From three to eight white eggs can be laid, but most clutches contain four or five. The incubation period is estimated at about 28 days, with the chore performed by both parents. The nestlings fledge when they are about 23 or 24 days old.

At their nests, Long-eared Owls sometimes engage in spectacular defensive behavior. For example, at nests in eastern Pennsylvania, the birds spread their wings as far as possible, snapped their bills to produce a clicking sound, and made numerous 113

The Long-eared Owl is sometimes confused with the larger and more powerful Great Horned Owl.

sounds which resembled the barking of a dog. When I climbed to the nests to examine their contents, the adult owls watched intently from a safe distance but did not try to strike me. They quickly returned to their nests after I had left the immediate vicinity.

One of the best (and most fascinating) ways to study owl food habits is by examining the pellets which these birds produce. These pellets are composed of fur, feathers, and bones of the prey they have eaten—material which the owls could not digest. Hence, they regurgitated or ejected the material in pellet form through their mouths. Unlike hawks, which tear or rip apart their prey, owls usually gulp their prey whole or in large chunks. Hence the bones and skulls of their prey usually can be recovered virtually intact by

A nestling Long-eared Owl in a pine woodlot in eastern Pennsylvania.

picking apart the contents of the pellets. In most cases, identification of the skeletal remains is relatively easy, particularly when entire skulls are recovered. Pellet analysis thus provides wildlife biologists and other interested persons with fascinating insights into the predation activities of owls.

Although various animals make occasional appearances in the diet of the Long-eared Owl, rodents unquestionably form a major proportion of the prey species captured—perhaps as much as 80 or 90 percent according to Arthur Cleveland Bent. Meadow Voles *(Microtus)* by far form the bulk of the prey in many instances. Mice of the genus *Peromyscus* also are taken frequently, along with rats, shrews, small birds, insects, and various other items. When birds are 115 captured, the owls usually have young in the nest to feed, and mice are relatively scarce. They then turn to alternative food sources which, in ecological terminology, are known as "buffer" species.

Short-eared Owl

The Short-eared Owl *(Asio flammeus)* is another species with a remarkably widespread distribution, being found on every continent except Australia. In North America, it occurs throughout the entire continent except the extreme northern parts of the Arctic. As breeding birds, Short-eared Owls primarily are confined to Canada and Alaska, but some have been found nesting as far south as New Jersey, northern Ohio, and southern Kansas. Their winter range more or less is confined to the contiguous United States.

The Short-eared Owl is one of the few owls which sometimes are active during the day, although it usually is seen flying over marshes or fields, hunting for food, at dawn or dusk. It has an irregular, flopping style of flight which resembles that of a nighthawk. This style of flight is a helpful field mark.

The habitat preferred by the Short-eared Owl is an open area such as tundra, marshes, grasslands, bushy areas, and dunes. The birds occasionally nest in small colonies. Typically, the nest is placed upon the ground in tall grasses where a shallow depression is prepared and lined with feathers, stubble, and straw.

Three to fourteen white eggs sometimes are laid, but four to seven form most clutches. The incubation period is said to be 21 to 23 days, but this probably is too short. The nestlings fledge when they are about 31 to 36 days old.

Field studies of the Short-eared Owl conducted by Richard Clark suggest that these birds are opportunistic in their breeding habits, and that the population density of voles during a given year may play an important role in regulating the breeding activities of the birds. When voles are abundant, the owls may breed, but when the rodents undergo a population crash and are scarce, Short-eared Owls may not breed. In fact, they may leave the area as a group and seek another location with a more abundant food supply. When the birds do nest, the number of eggs deposited varies depending upon the population level of the food. This seems to be a natural population control mechanism which helps to regulate the numbers of Short-eared Owls from season to season, and from region to region.

Several excellent studies have been made of the food habits of Short-eared Owls in the United States. For example, in one
Michigan study conducted by S. Arthur Reed, the contents of 111

pellets were studied. Voles and mice formed the total diet of the birds. Meadow Voles accounted for 74.1 percent of the prey captured, and mice of the genus *Peromyscus* the remaining 25.9 percent. And, in another Michigan study by Henry L. Short and Leslie C. Drew, *Microtus* voles and *Peromyscus* mice again formed the important food consumed by the owls.

Boreal Owl

One of the small, nocturnal owls confined almost entirely to the Canadian and Alaskan part of North America is the Boreal Owl *(Aegolius funereus)*. The species is separated into several subspecies. The American race sometimes is named the Richardson's Owl in the older literature, reflecting its scientific name *Aegolius funereus richardsoni*. Other subspecies occur in parts of Europe and Asia.

The Boreal Owl is about ten inches long. It lacks ear-tufts, has a relatively large head with light facial discs framed with black, and a yellow bill. The crown is spotted conspicuously with white, and the brown back has large white spots. The underparts are white to pale buff, with grayish-brown streaks on the breast and flanks. The eyes are yellow.

This is a bird of dense coniferous forests, particularly spruce forests, in the far North. It also occurs along the edges of such forests where mixed vegetation grows. It nests in small holes in trees, such as deserted woodpecker holes. From three to eight white eggs are laid, six forming a typical clutch. The incubation is performed entirely by the female and lasts for about 26 or 27 days. The nestlings fledge when they are about four or five weeks old.

The Boreal Owl rarely ventures far into the northern contiguous United States, but in its Alaskan and Canadian range it feeds upon a variety of small rodents, insects, and some birds. On the rare occasions when these owls do venture southward across the Canadian border, they do so because deep snows in their normal range cover mice runways and prevent the birds from obtaining food. Thus, most Boreal Owls which appear in the United States usually are starving, and many perish.

Saw-whet Owl

The Saw-whet Owl *(Aegolius acadicus)*, unlike the Boreal Owl, is strictly a North American species (with several subspecies recognized). Its vernacular name is derived from the sound of its voice, which resembles the sound made by the sharpening of a saw on an old-fashioned stone. This tiny owl, lacking ear-tufts, is only seven inches long. It also is unusually tame—one of its most notable characteristics. Adults are brown above with pale whitish streaks (not spots) on the crown, and pale brown streaking on the whitish underparts. Immatures are markedly different in appearance from adults. They are chocolate colored with a prominent white triangle between the yellow eyes. Individuals in this plumage seldom are seen as it is not retained for very long.

Saw-whet Owls are distributed widely throughout the southern half of Canada, and they occur as migrants and winter residents throughout most of the contiguous United States (except the southern third of the country). Nests have been found as far south as Missouri, Ohio, West Virginia, and Maryland. In the West, they nest in mountainous areas southward into Mexico. The birds are very shy and seldom are seen although they probably are far more common than our existing records suggest.

The habitat preferred by Saw-whet Owls is varied, generally being a forest, grove, or thicket. They usually select abandoned woodpecker holes or small natural cavities in trees in which to nest, but on Long Island, New York, one pair nested successfully in a bird box placed near the edge of a large salt marsh. Phragmites, poison ivy, and bayberry shrubs grew nearby.

Most clutches contain five or six white eggs, but sometimes four or seven are laid. They are incubated by the female for somewhat over 26 days. The nestlings fledge when they are about 27 to 34 days old.

The tiny Saw-whet Owl is one of the most interesting, but difficult to see, of our native owls. Not much larger than a man's hand, it is extremely tame and many individuals have been plucked by hand from their perches for banding purposes. Although these birds frequently roost on the lower branches of small pine trees, all of the individuals which I have seen were roosting amid the tangles of honeysuckle thickets. They usually were close to open fields and/or roads. The owls feed upon small mice and shrews, which form the bulk of their diet. Probably because of their hunting activities, Saw-whet Owls sometimes are found dead along roads during winter. Apparently they fly after mice and are struck by passing vehicles.

During autumn, Saw-whet Owls undergo definite migrations. Bird-banders sometimes catch them in their nets during this season of the year. Careful field studies also show that sizeable wintering populations sometimes occur in suitable areas.

11

RAPTOR ECOLOGY

Throughout the centuries, although many people have been inspired by hawks and owls, other people have not looked favorably upon these birds. The enactment by the Pennsylvania Legislature of the Scalp Act of 1885 is a case in point. Nor have people always understood the ecological importance of birds of prey despite careful scientific studies conducted during the past 150 years. The probable origin of western man's misunderstanding of the ecological importance of predators was explained by Robert Cushman Murphy of the American Museum of Natural History:

> The whole erroneous idea about control (meaning extermination) of predators arose in western Europe after man had to take charge of game management, as in English private "parks." In parts of the world where land use is still less artificial, as in Pennsylvania, a healthy supply of game birds, etc., depends upon a normal population of hawks, owls, and other predatory animals. They supply the basis upon which the welfare of life as a whole depends.
>
> The Azores Islands were named for hawks. It is very interesting that even today these islands have an extraordinarily large population of hawks, chiefly *Buteo*, and that along with them quail, woodcock, and vast numbers of small birds abound. The situation represents nature in proper balance.

The purpose of the English game parks was to provide good hunting sport. Anything tending to eliminate some game was considered undesirable. Since birds of prey kill some game animals, they were viewed as "vermin" which should be destroyed. Yet recent field studies show that predatory birds often are only about 7 or 8 119 percent successful in their hunting attempts. Nonetheless, hawks and owls were resented. To the game managers, the obvious answer was to eliminate predators. Presumably that would produce more game and better hunting.

The theory seemed logical. But it ignored several fundamental ecological processes which function within all animal communities. For example, a plot of land contains limited quantities of food, water, and cover resources useful to wildlife. They establish the land's carrying capacity. If too many animals compete for the same food and shelter, or attempt to live on the same area, overcrowding results and the area's carrying capacity is exceeded. Perhaps all of the animals will survive, but some are forced to live on poorer parts of the land and to eat poorer, less palatable, or more inaccessible food. Some animals also may be more vulnerable to predators such as hawks and owls than are others living in spots with the best food and cover.

In addition to not understanding the concept of carrying capacity, the game managers also were unaware that hawks and owls commonly (but not always) capture and kill surplus, weak, or diseased animals. In many instances these are animals which have exceeded the land's carrying capacity. In general, it is surplus, weak, or sick animals which form the bulk of the diet of birds of prey.

Sometimes birds of prey also are responsible for *increasing* rather than decreasing wildlife populations. One of the best examples of this type of wildlife interaction concerns the ecological roles of Northern Goshawks and Cooper's Hawks nesting in the forests of northern Pennsylvania and New York.

Field studies on these birds were conducted by Heinz Meng. During a ten-year period, detailed observations were made at many Cooper's and Northern Goshawk nests. In the Ithaca, New York, region the food of adult and nestling Cooper's Hawks from 12 broods consisted of 18 percent mammals and 82 percent birds. The most important prey mammals, Eastern Chipmunks and Red Squirrels, formed 94 percent of the mammalian diet during the raptor breeding season. Of the birds consumed, 87 percent consisted of European Starlings, Common Flickers, Eastern Meadowlarks, American Robins, and Common Grackles. European Starlings were by far, the most frequently captured and eaten. Observations at nests provided additional information regarding the amount of predation pressure which the hawks placed upon the various prey species. The feeding activities at a typical Cooper's Hawk nest provide a case in point. Meng reported:

In a typical nest containing four young, an average of 266 prey items was brought to the nest during the first six weeks: 4 quarries per day during the first week, 5 per day during the second week, 7 per day throughout the third week, 9 per day during the fourth week, 7 each day during the fifth week and 6 per day in the sixth week. It takes an average of 66 prey items to raise a Cooper's hawk to the age of six weeks. The females are about one-third larger than the males and require more food, so this figure would be slightly higher for the females and lower for the males.

Equally interesting, most of the Cooper's Hawks' prey consisted of young, inexperienced animals. Only occasionally were adult animals captured—presumably while protecting their young. At times even nestlings two-thirds grown were taken. This information permitted a fuller understanding of the ecological role which the Cooper's Hawk plays in helping to regulate some songbird populations. The hawks were vital participants in the food webs which existed within their nesting and hunting territories.

In addition to the studies of nesting Cooper's Hawks, comparative studies also were made at fourteen Northern Goshawk nests in New York and northern Pennsylvania. These birds are the largest and most powerful accipitrine hawks in North America. Doubtless they were the most powerful and highest trophic (feeding) level raptors in the areas where they nested. Information was carefully gathered at the nests, and it refuted many long-held ideas about the role which Northern Goshawks play in relation to grouse populations. For years people had accused them of killing large numbers of Ruffed Grouse, thereby ruining grouse hunting. One recent midwestern study seemed to confirm this viewpoint. Yet the studies in Pennsylvania and New York demonstrated that grouse were common in areas where Northern Goshawks nested. But only five grouse were taken as prey. In comparison, 83 crows were captured, along with 58 Red Squirrels, and a variety of other birds and mammals.

When the ecological roles and behavior of all of the Northern Goshawk prey were carefully considered, some remarkable insights into the ecological importance of these accipiters were obtained. For example, it was clear that Northern Goshawks in New York and Pennsylvania forests do not select a particular area for nesting because of high grouse populations. Indeed, they probably are instrumental in helping grouse populations to *increase* rather than to decrease. "Red squirrels, chipmunks, and crows destroy many grouse nests by feeding on the eggs and young, or, as in the case of the chipmunk, by pushing the eggs out of the nest," reported Meng. Thus, by helping to control important predators of grouse, the hawks actually help to increase the numbers of these gamebirds.

Careful studies of other species of hawks in different habitats and areas also demonstrate the value of these pedators. My field studies of nesting American Kestrels in eastern Pennsylvania provide a case in point. These kestrels are the smallest and most colorful falcons in North America. They generally live in open areas such as fields, meadows, and farming districts. Some also have adapted to life in towns and cities and nest successfully close to human activity.

My field studies were made in an agricultural area. During an eight-year period, 21 active kestrel nests were located on a Berks County farm. To avoid unnecessary disturbance, only 14 nests were studied in varying degrees of completeness. All were in special wood boxes placed in suitable locations. Of 55 eggs laid, 43 (78 percent) hatched.

Interesting as these figures are, the food habits of the kestrels during spring and summer demonstrated that the falcons were important ecological members of the wildlife community. For example, during a four-year period, 271 prey items were analyzed revealing that the prolific Meadow Vole *(Microtus)* was the single most important animal captured and consumed. Voles are serious destroyers of many crops. But, at the same time, they are preyed upon heavily by many species of hawks and owls. Ground beetles and a few birds also formed a portion of the diet of the kestrels. Clearly, these birds played important roles in helping to control the numbers of some of the most prolific and abundant animals in the food chains and food webs of this farming district.

Although the list of prey taken by the kestrels is interesting, the ecological interactions of the falcons upon an explosive population of Periodical Cicadas *(Magicicada septendecim)* was of exceptional interest. The cicadas were forest insects whereas the kestrels were birds of open fields and farmlands. Thus the two species essentially were restricted to separate (but adjacent) habitats. A few cicadas spilled into the fields near the edge of the forest, however, and occasionally a kestrel entered the forest's edge. Ecologists refer to an area containing vegetation characteristics of two different, but adjacent, habitats as an "edge" or "ecotone." On the Berks County site, the forest edge was poorly defined since there was an abrupt change from forest to field. Nonetheless, enough cicadas ventured into the open fields, and enough kestrels entered the forest edge with sufficient frequency, to permit some cicadas to be captured by the falcons. Thus, in 1962, the only year during which the cicadas were present (they appear only once during every seventeen years), these insects formed 16.5 percent of the kestrel's diet.

This interaction between falcons and cicadas illustrates several additional ecological principles. For example, in order for a predator to capture an animal, the animal must be available *and* vulnerable. It must not only live in an area in which a predator hunts, it also must occur in a situation which will allow it to be captured. In the case of the kestrels and cicadas, the insects primarily were potential prey species. Generally they were not vulnerable to the falcons in any significant degree because they lived in a habitat not very well sutied for kestrel hunting techniques.

This example also illustrates another important ecological principle—all animals require specific habitats in which to live. Seldom does an animal leave that habitat for extended periods, except during migration or because of some unusual circumstance. In Berks County, Pennsylvania, the role of the kestrels was to help to control the numbers of field rodents and insects. An occasional bird was captured if it was available and vulnerable.

The Berks County, Pennsylvania, habitat where American Kestrels were studied by the author.

Many additional examples could be cited to illustrate the ecological importance of birds of prey. In Georgia, for example, Sharp-shinned and Cooper's Hawks preyed upon Bobwhites, but other raptors either were beneficial or neutral. The Northern Harrier is a case in point. Harriers fed heavily upon Cotton Rats, a common rodent in the area. The rats were known to destroy many quail eggs. Thus it seems that Northern Harriers helped to maintain, if not actually increase, local Bobwhite populations by eliminating numbers of destructive rats. A delicate and effective ecological balance between predator and prey was at work—a balance which man could readily alter if he attempted to kill birds of prey.

Thus far only the ecological roles of several species of diurnal birds of prey have been discussed. It also is appropriate to consider the predatory activities of several species of nocturnal birds of prey—the owls. There are many important field studies of owls reported upon by wildlife biologists, but two are particularly famous.

The first of these concerns the predation ecology of Great Horned Owls in the north central part of the United States. It was conducted in Wisconsin and Iowa by Paul L. Errington, Frances Hamerstrom, and F. N. Hamerstrom, Jr. The field study extended over a period of five years, involved the collection of data at 84

In Georgia, one study showed that Northern Harriers preyed upon Cotton Rats which were destructive to quail eggs. Photo by Fred Tilly.

In Wisconsin and Iowa one study showed that Great Horned Owls captured whatever prey was available, although medium-sized mammals formed the staple diet of the owls.   125

horned owl nests, and included examination of the contents of 4,815 pellets and 23 food-containing owl stomachs. The pellet analysis was an especially valuable study technique.

The information which was gathered was particularly complete for the colder half of the year, but less so for the warmer half. For the most part, Great Horned Owls were found to be opportunistic in their predatory activities. Whatever suitable prey happened to be most easily secured was captured. Some differences occurred in the diets of the owls, however. These resulted primarily from variations in ecological conditions related to season and geographic location. Nonetheless, cottontails, hares, and other medium-sized mammals formed the greater part (up to almost 70 percent by volume) of the staple prey of the Great Horned Owls. Mice, other small mammals, and resident birds, were somewhat less important as prey. Various other migratory birds, lower vertebrates, and invertebrates also were preyed upon occasionally. The three biologists concluded:

> On the whole, it seems doubtful if north-central horned owls and associated predators exert a dominant influence upon populations of prey animals taken. The predators, even in numbers as great as many may themselves tolerate or can maintain locally, seldom appear to utilize more than a small proportion of the staple foods, i.e., rabbits and mice, conveniently available to them and, as a rule, turn to other mammals or to birds when these temporarily become more available than the prey staples. Over-population of habitats by nonstaple prey species has been accompanied by some of the most pronounced rises in representation of these types in diets of such flesh-eaters as the horned owl; crises precipitated by weather, destruction of environment, human activities, etc., were often reflected, as well, by response of predators to increased vulnerability of given prey animals.
>
> Predator-prey relationships studied in the north-central region were flexible, and predators did not always respond to apparent changes in availability of prey. Nevertheless, unrelieved basic insecurities of prey populations were often attended by response of some predators sufficient to compensate, at least in part, for lack of utilization by others; and compensatory tendencies in loss rates of prey animals were noted under a wide range of conditions having little evident connection with kinds and densities of predators.

The second famous study dealt with Barn Owls living in the vicinity of East Lansing, Michigan. It lasted for three years and was conducted by George J. Wallace. To examine the predation activities of these birds, as reflected by skeletal remains of prey preserved in pellets, 2,200 Barn Owl pellets from two sites were analyzed. Although a total of 6,815 prey animals were represented in the pellets, it was the percentage of representation of the various prey species which was extraordinarily fascinating. The Meadow Vole *(Microtus pennsylvanicus)* averaged almost 85 percent of all prey consumed during the three years the investigation continued. However, the percentage of *Microtus* showed considerable seasonal and yearly variation. At one point, for example, it dropped to only 57 percent of the diet whereas during another period it accounted for almost 97 percent of all food eaten by the Barn Owls. Since these voles exhibit periodic population cycles, i.e., "explosions" and "crashes" in numbers, it is likely that the different percentages of *Microtus* represented in the diets of the Barn Owls reflected cyclic phenomena of their staple food item.

In addition to the vast numbers of *Microtus* captured by the owls, deer mice of the genus *Peromyscus* averaged about 4.5 percent of their diet, Meadow Jumping Mice *(Zapus hudsonius)* 1.17 percent, and Short-tailed Shrews *(Blarina brevicauda)* another 6.53 percent. A variety of other small mammals, and a few birds, formed the remainder of the diet of Barn Owls at East Lansing, Michigan. It is obvious from these data that Barn Owls are very important ecological components of those Michigan ecosystems which support large populations of voles of the genus *Microtus*. Although many predators feed to a greater or lesser degree upon these small mammals, few predators feed upon the rodents as regularly, and in such large quantities, as do Barn Owls. Apparently the two species are linked in what is nearly an inseparable predator food chain.

In view of the important roles which birds of prey play in helping to maintain the balance of nature, it is ironic that the food habits of raptors remained poorly known until less than 150 years ago. During the latter part of the last century, however, interest developed in the economic roles of raptors in agricultural activities, and ornithologists carefully examined the contents of thousands of stomachs of hawks and owls taken from all parts of the United States, examined the contents of pellets, and noted the food which was carried to hawk and owl nests by the parent birds.

Perhaps the most famous of these pioneer studies was done by A. K. Fisher. He published his data in a book issued by the United States Department of Agriculture entitled *The Hawks and Owls of the United States in their Relation to Agriculture.* This book was a landmark in efforts to provide a better scientific understanding of birds of prey. The research demonstrated that the vast majority of predatory birds are of considerable economic benefit to man and, when the total ecological roles of predators are considered, all hawks and owls are of enormous importance in helping to maintain the balance of nature.

Interesting as food habit studies are, they nonetheless have some weaknesses built into them. For example, the food eaten by raptors in one locality during one season frequently differs from the dietary habits of the same species living in other areas or during

127

another season. Thus food habit studies generally reveal average diets and are not intended to predict what a specific individual will eat.

A far more satisfactory way to look at the role of birds of prey is to consider and attempt to understand how these predators fit into the overall scheme of nature. This is the modern ecological approach. To employ this method, it first is necessary to discard previous ideas which may suggest that hawks and owls are good or bad. All animals (and plants) have important roles to play in nature's web of life; each is important to the ecological welfare of animal and plant communities. Sometimes one animal may appear to man to be more important than another, but it is ecologically impossible to consider any living creature as "good" or "bad."

Sometimes it is difficult to consider hawks and owls objectively because they are carnivores or flesh-eating animals. They kill to survive, and some people are shocked by such apparent brutality. They try to apply human moral judgments to wild animals. But when they stop and consider that they, too, are meat-eaters, they develop a better understanding of predation as a vital and dynamic force in nature.

Generally raptors kill and eat the smaller and more plentiful animals—at least insofar as predation in North America is concerned. Many animals killed by hawks and owls already have eaten still smaller animals. Thus, from an ecological viewpoint, a step by step or chain-like series of events is created whereby larger and less numerous predators eat smaller and more plentiful animals. This is called a predator food chain or merely a food chain. Each link in the chain serves as food for animals which form the next higher link. Moreover, since all life must obtain energy to sustain itself, this needed energy is transferred from one link in the food chain to the next higher link via an ecological process known as "energy flow."

Armed with this background information, it is not difficult to understand why hawks and owls are essential members of the biotic communities in which they live. Keeping in mind the food habits of various raptors, it is interesting to examine in more detail several food chains to see how they are formed and how they work.

The first is a food chain in an eastern forest, the second in a small woodlot, and the third in an old field. Although different plants and animals form the chains, the same principles apply to each and, in fact, to all food chains regardless of their length.

In the first example, vegetation (flowers, shrubs, vines, and trees) forms the food chain's base because it manufactures food from carbon dioxide and water in combination with energy from the sun. Ecologists therefore consider plants as producers. Next,

plant-eating insects appear. They commonly are the first animals to
eat food manufactured by plants. Insects, therefore, are called first
order consumers or herbivores. However, not all primary or first
order consumers are as tiny as insects. The White-tailed Deer, with a
biomass (size and weight) far in excess of an insect, also is a
herbivore. All first order consumers are essential members of food
chains because they convert plant tissue into animal protein suitable
for consumption by animals higher in the food chain. In our
northern forest, for example, wood warblers are common birds. But
they cannot utilize plant foods directly. Instead, they eat insects
which have eaten plants. Thus wood warblers are second order
consumers. They indirectly obtain energy originally mobilized by
plants. The next link in our forest food chain is the Sharp-shinned
Hawk. Smaller than the powerful Northern Goshawk, to which it is
related, the Sharp-shin occupies a third order position in the chain
of animal feeders. It is a third order consumer. This hawk feeds
upon small, forest-dwelling birds such as thrushes, vireos, and wood
warblers. It receives its energy third-hand—by eating birds which
have eaten insects which have eaten plants.

The next food chain example deals with some of the plants and
animals living in a woodlot. Similar ecological principles apply to
these food chains. The producers are flowers, vines, shrubs, and
trees. Ants and other insects form the first order consumers. The
Common Flicker, a common woodpecker, is a second order
consumer, whereas the larger Cooper's Hawk is a third order
consumer and final link in this particular food chain.

The third example is illustrated by the Barn Owls and
American Kestrels which live in the agricultural districts of eastern
Pennsylvania. Grasses and other plants of the fields and meadows
of this region are the producers. The prolific Meadow Vole, which
feeds largely upon grasses, is the first order consumer. The kestrels
and Barn Owls then enter the food chain as second order
consumers. They frequently represent the end of the food chain. But
if larger predators (such as Red-tailed Hawks) happen to be present
and add another link to the chain they become third order
consumers.

Those predators far removed from the plant producers receive
only a tiny portion of the energy stored in plants. Much is wasted
while being transferred from consumer to consumer. Therefore
there must be larger numbers of producers but fewer consumers.
Additionally, food chains are not endless. Some contain only one or
two steps; others have five or more links. In general, long food
chains are inefficient and rare because too much energy is wasted
while being transferred from animal to animal.

These three examples illustrate how hawks and owls fit into   129

A male American Kestrel hovering above a field searching for a Meadow Vole.

food chains. Still, that is only part of the story. Rarely do isolated food chains exist in biotic communities. Usually they are interconnected into food webs. Not uncommonly, an animal is a member of several food chains at once, depending upon its position in a food web. Almost all food webs are extremely complex, which is unfortunate because it makes them extremely difficult to study and understand. Indeed, only the most simple, such as those in polar regions, are completely understood. Food webs operating in most North American forests, woodlots, fields, and meadows still are incompletely investigated. Nonetheless, enough information exists to provide ecologists with a reasonably adequate understanding of their operation and environmental importance.

From the information which is available, one fact is clear. An adequate understanding of birds of prey can only be achieved by considering an area's entire raptor (hawk and owl) population in relation to the food and space utilized, the raptors' daily and seasonal movements, and many other critically related factors. Few such field studies have been made. One of the best, requiring four years of intensive investigation on a 36-square-mile area in

Washtenaw County, Michigan, was completed by John J. Craighead and Frank C. Craighead, Jr. They published the results of their study in *Hawks, Owls and Wildlife,* which every raptor enthusiast should read. Leslie Brown also provides similar information on African raptor ecology in *African Birds of Prey.*

The field studies which John and Frank Craighead conducted give ecologists important insights into the complex roles which hawks and owls play in the balance of nature. For example, no single species of hawk or owl catches and kills members of all of the potential prey species in an area. But when the entire raptor population is considered collectively, all of the species of hawks and owls could do so. The predation pressure which a population of breeding raptors exerts upon prey is applied in three important ways. First, there are critical periods during which pressure is applied. Second, the maximum pressure which is applied occurs when prey density also reaches maximum levels. Usually this is during spring, immediately following the breeding season. And, third, birds of prey apply continuous, but proportionate, pressure upon a collective prey population.

The Craigheads' field studies also afforded some additional ecological insights into daily and seasonal activities of hawks and owls. The Craigheads discovered, for example, that raptors (along with other predators) establish and maintain a balance or equilibrium among animal populations. Raptor predation operates according to definite patterns. The birds hunt where prey is most abundant and vulnerable, thus resulting in the most abundant prey being captured in proportion to their abundance. For example, if voles form 75 percent of the total available prey for a collective population of hawks and owls, mice of the genus *Peromyscus* 11 percent, game birds eight percent, and small birds six percent, each of these animals more or less will be represented in similar percentages in the collective (combined) raptor kill for the area under study.

Equipped with this ecological background, we can understand why hawks and owls, and predators in general, play extremely vital roles in biotic communities. We should also be able to understand why it is ecologically unwise to attempt to increase the populations of one species (usually game animals) by eliminating predators. Invariably, efforts of this type fail because they ignore basic ecological principles. They create unbalanced environments which frequently lead to extreme fluctuations in the populations of some animals such as rodents. If populations of game animals must be increased to satisfy the demands of hunters, habitat preservation and improvement usually is the only really effective and acceptable management technique. Similar techniques also can be used for nongame wildlife resources.

The Dutch ornithologist K. H. Voous pointed out that when considering the wildlife resources on an area, it is important to remember that birds of prey are excellent and inexpensive indicator species (biometers) reflecting an area's ecological diversity and environmental health. Birds of prey serve as good biometers for several reasons. First, they are large and easily observed. Second, when numerous *common* birds of prey live on an area they demonstrate the presence of a healthy assortment of plants and animals in various habitats. The raptors would not be common, or present at all, if the necessary plant and wildlife diversity upon which they depend for survival was not present. Thus Voous urges conservationists to take special measures to protect areas with a rich assortment of common birds of prey *because* the raptors are common. If enough such conservation efforts supporting common birds of prey are augmented, there is the probability that some future costly and/or controversial defensive actions (which are really last minute efforts) in endangered species programs will not be needed. The idea is simple: Save species when they are common.

12
HAWK MIGRATIONS

During spring and autumn, hawks migrate to or from their North American breeding grounds in large numbers. Frequently, particularly during autumn, these birds concentrate at various locations because of the natural topographic features which exist there. Some notable bottlenecks for migrating hawks occur along parts of the Atlantic coastline, along certain inland mountains which usually extend relatively unbroken for long distances in northeasterly to southwesterly directions, and along the northern and western shorelines of the Great Lakes.

When migrating hawks reach these spots, thousands sometimes are counted in a single day, making these flights among the most spectacular animal migrations found anywhere in the world. Recently, in the West, fairly large numbers of migrating hawks also have been counted in autumn in the San Francisco Bay area.

To enjoy and appreciate hawk migrations fully, it is rewarding to visit some lookouts used by hawk watchers during the migration seasons. I provide directions for visiting many such sites in *A Guide to Hawk Watching in North America* and more detailed technical information about hawk migrations in the East in *Autumn Hawk Flights*. Binoculars are absolutely necessary for visitors to a hawk lookout, to see the migrating birds clearly.

Spring Migrations

In many respects spring hawk migrations are quite different from those that occur during autumn. In spring, the hawks generally are more widespread and do not seem to concentrate at various geographic bottlenecks as readily as the birds do in autumn. Nevertheless, some spring concentration points are known. The most important are in southern Texas and along the south shorelines of Lakes Erie and Ontario, but others occur at a few spots along the Atlantic coastline and elsewhere.

Apparently hawks migrating northward dislike crossing large bodies of water. Therefore, when they reach major geographic features such as the Great Lakes they divert their migration route eastward along the southern shorelines of these lakes. The largest concentrations usually occur where bays or water inlets occur, and where land extends into the lakes just west of the sites used as lookouts. According to John Haugh, who made a careful study of these migrations, when hawks encounter the waters of inlets as they are moving eastward they avoid crossing those waters and turn and follow the shoreline toward the southeast. Because other hawks migrating overland a mile or more from the main waters of the lakes also encounter waters from the inlets, flight lines at such locations tend to become narrower along the embayed areas. This results in concentrations of hawks. Large numbers of birds can sometimes be counted.

Other topographic features also can influence migrating hawks as they pass along lake shorelines. For example, when open-country hawks such as harriers encounter woodlands they sometimes divert their flight path to cross over open fields. Similarly, at locations where open fields border lake shorelines, accipters may fly inland over woodlands or follow along the boundaries of woodlands and fields. Knowledge of the preferred habitats of various species of hawks sometimes can aid observers in locating the best spots to watch the birds during migration.

Weather conditions are important and influential factors affecting both spring and autumn hawk migrations in a variety of ways. In spring, for example, hawk flights seem to occur most frequently when southerly winds, a rise in air temperature, falling barometric pressure, and a low-pressure area and cold front approach from a westerly direction. By looking for these conditions as they are reported in newspapers or on television weather reports, one sometimes can predict the occurrence of good spring hawk flights.

The bulk of the spring hawk migrations occur during March, April, and May. Mid- to late April is particularly favorable for

seeing substantial numbers of Sharp-shinned and Broad-winged
Hawks at a few sites along the south shorelines of Lakes Erie and
Ontario.

Autumn Migrations

Autumn is by far the most exciting season to observe large
numbers of migrating hawks. Tens of thousands of birds then
migrate southward. Although a trickle of birds begin to appear
early in August, and a few continue flying into early December,
most of the flights occur during September, October, and
November. It is during these months that visits to many of the hawk
lookouts are worthwhile. Indeed, in recent years more and more
people have discovered just how exciting and worthwhile such visits
can be.

September, especially, is noted for spectacular migrations of
Broad-winged Hawks. Not infrequently these birds appear in largest
numbers (sometimes thousands appear in a single day) around the
16th or 17th of September at famous lookouts such as Hawk
Mountain, Pennsylvania. During some years, however, peak
Broad-wing flights occur somewhat earlier or a little later but rarely
more than a week or so.

A large flight of migrating Broad-winged Hawks truly is
spectacular. As many as 600 or more of these small soaring hawks
mill around in swirling "kettles" in seemingly endless confusion
inside a thermal (a large, invisible bubble of warm air rising into the
atmosphere). It is not unusual to count 2,000 or 3,000 Broad-wings
on a peak flight day at many lookouts, and occasionally flights of
10,000 or more birds have been reported from a few locations. The
most spectacular flight reported at Hawk Mountain in eastern
Pennsylvania, for example, took place on 16 September 1948, when
11,392 hawks (mostly Broad-wings) were counted. Occasionally
even larger flights occur at spots along the Great Lakes. At the
Hawk Ridge Nature Reserve in Duluth, Minnesota, for example,
approximately 24,000 Broad-winged Hawks were counted on 22
September 1970! Great Lakes concentration points in southern
Ontario (e.g., Hawk Cliff, Point Pelee, and Holiday Beach
Provincial Park) also produce similarly large hawk flights at times.
Bald Eagles also fly southward in small numbers during late August
and September although their migrations also continue in limited
numbers during the entire season. Ospreys, too, usually reach peak
numbers during mid- to late September, although on 11 September
1965, at Bake Oven Knob, Pennsylvania, I counted 102 of these
splendid birds passing the lookout.

In many respects, October is even more exciting than   135

During migration Broad-winged Hawks frequently form flocks or kettles in thermals. Sometimes these kettles contain hundreds of birds.

Turkey Vultures are observed commonly in autumn at many eastern hawk lookouts.

September to many hawk watchers. There is always something to observe then. At many of the lookouts the autumn foliage reaches its peak of color in mid- to late October, adding a spectacular backdrop to the migrating hawks. Moreover, a wide variety of migrating waterfowl and songbirds also appear during October. Thus birds ranging in size from tiny kinglets, vireos, and wood warblers to large soaring birds such as majestic Golden Eagles combine to add interest to bird watching from many sites. Sharp-shinned Hawks, in particular, pass southward in large numbers during early to mid-October. Sometimes hundreds of these small accipiters can be counted in a single day at various Great Lakes, Appalachian mountain, and Atlantic coastal lookouts. Other spectacular birds such as Cooper's Hawks, Merlins and Peregrine Falcons also appear in these migrations in limited numbers, increasing the excitement of the birding. Canada Geese

An immature Cooper's Hawk migrating past a hawk lookout in October. Photo by Fred Tilly.

also appear in large numbers, and occasionally Whistling Swans and Snow Geese are observed.

From late October into November many large and spectacular hawks pass the hawk lookouts in memorable numbers. For example, just about any cold and windy day in early November should produce many Red-tailed Hawks soaring southward. Often lesser numbers of other raptors such as Red-shouldered Hawks, Northern Goshawks, Golden Eagles, and an occasional Rough-legged Hawk are seen. Still other species which pass southward during this time include such species as Cooper's Hawks, Northern Harriers, a late Bald Eagle or Osprey, or very rarely a Gyrfalcon.

To appreciate fully what the best hawk lookouts in eastern North America can offer to persons interested in seeing these wildlife spectacles, one must visit them on suitable days. Just as weather plays very important roles in determining when large spring hawk flights occur, so too does weather play similar roles in

An immature eastern Red-tailed Hawk hanging in mid-air over a hawk lookout. Photo by Fred Tilly.

The white rump of this Northern Harrier is visible as the bird migrates past a hawk lookout and is an important field mark for this species. Photo by Fred Tilly.

governing when autumn hawk flights occur at the various locations. Generally a good rule of thumb to follow when selecting a day on which to visit a lookout is to note from weather reports when a low-pressure area covers lower New England and upstate New York coupled with the passage of a brisk cold front moving across the East. That day, or sometimes the next, clear skies and brisk westerly or northwesterly winds should occur. In the Northeast, such winds strike the sides of the Appalachian Mountains and create excellent updrafts. Soaring hawks make extensive use of these air currents as they migrate along various sections of the Appalachian chain. Other birds follow the Great Lakes shorelines, or the Atlantic coastline southward and frequently become concentrated at natural geographic bottlenecks.

Some of the hawks observed passing the various hawk lookouts travel very long distances to their wintering grounds. For example, Ospreys and Broad-winged Hawks winter in Central or South America. Other species such as Golden Eagles travel much shorter distances and winter in the southern Appalachians, insofar as the eastern eagles are concerned, or in the Southwest in the case of many migratory western Golden Eagles. Many Bald Eagles migrating down the Mississippi River or wintering along various sections of that great waterway return in spring to Canada and perhaps Alaska to nest.

Most of the Bald Eagles observed passing sites such as Hawk Mountain, Pennsylvania, are Florida birds returning from their summer range in the Northeast to various sections of Florida where they nest from November to March. Many Peregrine Falcons, however, nest in the Arctic and winter well into South America. Thus the distances traveled each year by birds of prey vary considerably depending upon which species is in question. All, however, are worthwhile sights.

Hawk Lookouts

It is not possible in this short chapter to describe all the excellent hawk lookouts now used by hawk watchers in North America or to give full details about the many sites. The books mentioned earlier in this chapter provide such information. But it is useful here to discuss briefly a few of the more important and better known sites.

In New England in autumn, hawk watchers have used Goat Peak in Mount Tom State Reservation near Springfield, Massachusetts, for many years. Observations are made from a steel tower. Along coastal Connecticut, at New Haven, Lighthouse Point Park is another popular lookout. In New York State an outstanding spring lookout, Derby Hill, is located along the southeastern shoreline of Lake Ontario near the town of Mexico. Hook Mountain, another lookout in New York State, is mainly an autumn observation site. It is located just north of Nyack overlooking the Hudson River.

New Jersey also has some excellent autumn hawk lookouts. The most famous and important is Cape May Point at the extreme southern tip of the state. In autumn, thousands of migrating birds, including songbirds and hawks, are seen here on favorable days (especially when northwest winds occur). Indeed the Point is one of the most beautiful and important bird concentration areas in North America and thousands of bird watchers annually visit there.

Cape May Point, New Jersey, is a major autumn hawk lookout.

Hawk watchers on the North Lookout at Hawk Mountain Sanctuary in eastern Pennsylvania. This is the most famous site in North America for observing migrating hawks.

Nearby, in Pennsylvania, there are many very important spots from which migrating hawks can be seen. Hawk Mountain, near Kempton, is by far the most famous because it was the first wildlife sanctuary in North America established to protect migrating hawks. The story of its creation, vividly described by Maurice Broun in *Hawks Aloft,* is one of the outstanding chapters in American wildlife conservation. Bake Oven Knob, near Hawk Mountain, is another outstanding hawk lookout in eastern Pennsylvania.

Along the northern and western shorelines of the Great Lakes are additional important hawk lookouts. One of the best, Hawk Ridge Nature Reserve, is located in Duluth, Minnesota. Bird watchers from far and near use its lookouts every autumn.

Sometimes, in spring, impressive hawk migrations also are seen in southern Texas as the birds enter the United States from
Mexico. The area in the vicinity of Santa Ana National Wildlife

Refuge near the town of Alamo sometimes can be very productive. Point Diablo, near San Francisco, California, also is a worthwhile autumn hawk lookout. Lesser numbers of hawks also are seen there in spring.

North Americans are not alone in their interest and appreciation of hawk migrations. Many European hawk watchers now visit several outstanding concentration areas in Europe and the Middle East; there is another important site in the vicinity of the Panama Canal; and it seems likely that some important sites still are undiscovered. Interested persons are searching for such places throughout the world in order to gather new information on hawk migrations, to enjoy the flights, and to preserve some of the more important locations as special refuges or natural areas.

Hawk watchers on the South Lookout at Bake Oven Knob, Pennsylvania.

13

OWL
MIGRATIONS

In contrast to the spectacular migrations of hawks, which attract thousands of naturalists and birders to numerous eastern North American observation points, owl migrations are little noticed and difficult to study. Because owls are nocturnal, we cannot establish lookouts from which migrating birds can be seen and counted. Instead, information must be collected bit by bit, over long periods of time, and only after intensive efforts are made hunting for and banding the birds. Without bird-banding, it is unlikely that the seasonal movements of owls could be studied effectively.

The results of such studies are rewarding. Recoveries of banded birds demonstrate that some species are very migratory. Some examples are Barn, Snowy, and Saw-whet Owls. Other owls also have some migratory movements, or at least move around from time to time, especially during winter. It is likely that some of these limited movements are correlated with marked changes in food supply. Other environmental factors which may cause owls to migrate are not well understood.

Barn Owl

In the case of the Barn Owl, lows in vole *(Microtus)* populations probably are related to some migrations by these birds—at least in the northern United States. Unusually cold winter weather also may cause some birds to migrate southward. It is

The geographic movements of Barn Owls banded as nestlings and recovered 100 miles or more from the locations where they were hatched. Banding sites are indicated by circles, recovery sites by triangles. From Stewart (1952) in The Auk.

known that definite Barn Owl migrations occur, at least among the birds forming the northern population. After carefully studying 336 Barn Owl banding recoveries. Paul A. Stewart discovered that a line drawn through 35° N. separated Barn Owls into two groups. The southern group was relatively sedentary, but a significant displacement occurred among birds in the northern group. Both young and adult individuals were involved in these migrations. Moreover, the migrations involved southward flights in autumn and northward flights in spring.

Stewart also discovered that Barn Owls returned north to within 200 miles of their hatching places by the first of April. Some individuals then continued their northward migration within the 200-mile zone through April. Not until mid-April or early May did the last of the owls complete their migrations.

An impressive difference between the average life span of the northern and southern owls also occurred. The life span of 70 southern birds was two years, two months, and 26 days. That of the 145

150 northern birds was one year, one month, and four days. Dangers encountered during migration probably accounted for the shorter lives of the northern birds.

Interesting as this information is, a great deal of additional information still is needed before Barn Owl migrations will be understood completely. In Eastern Pennsylvania, for example, some owls are migratory during winter and do not return until March. But other individuals are nonmigratory and have nested in October and January. Owls, it seems, indeed are mysterious creatures.

Snowy Owl

The Snowy Owl is a large, handsome bird which normally lives in the Arctic and sub-Arctic where it feeds mainly upon lemmings and other small rodents. Its migrations are less regular than those of some other species such as Barn Owls. This is primarily related to its food habits, for the owls are only forced southward in large numbers about every four years. These migrations sometimes are called invasions. When lemmings are very abundant, there is no need for Snowy Owls to migrate. But when the little rodents become very scarce, as they do every few years, the owls are forced to seek other sources of food. The birds then migrate southward.

However, the periodic cycles which characterize lemming populations do not occur at the same time over wide geographic areas. Therefore, a few Snowy Owls, representing geographic areas of limited size, migrate southward almost yearly and appear in the northern contiguous United States. But the very large Snowy Owl invasions, which frequently involve hundreds if not thousands of birds, only occur when lemmings happen to be scarce over widespread sections of the Arctic.

Alfred O. Gross, who studied Snowy Owl invasion data carefully, concluded that these birds invaded the eastern United States with regularity about every four years. Since 1882, the intervals between invasions stood at four of three years, nine of four years, and three of five years up to the 1945-46 invasion.

So, when Snowy Owls do migrate well into the United States they are special Arctic visitors. And more and more people are learning to appreciate and enjoy the birds rather than to shoot them as has been done so often in the past. Fortunately, all birds of prey now are fully protected by federal laws.

Saw-whet Owl

Recent studies of Saw-whet Owls suggest that these tiny birds are far more common during autumn, winter, and spring than was suspected previously. However, the birds are very difficult to detect, even at close range, and therefore they are frequently overlooked. For example, on several occasions I found these owls roosting in honeysuckle thickets but was unable to see the birds until someone pointed them out to me. And I was only three feet from the birds! Their superb protective coloration and ability to remain motionless and blend into their surroundings are extraordinary.

The best way to study the migrations of Saw-whet Owls, therefore, is to look at the recoveries of banded birds. In one recent study in the eastern half of North America some specific migration patterns became evident after the banding recovery records were studied. Spring migrations, which are less well known than autumn migrations, occur from March through May whereas the autumn migration begins in late September and continues into late November in New York and New Jersey. Mid to late October is the peak migration period.

The banding recoveries also show that Saw-whet Owls use two distinct migration routes in eastern North America. One route begins in central Ontario and extends southwestward through the Ohio River Valley to Kentucky. The other route is the Atlantic coastline from Maine southward to North Carolina. Apparently the birds use much the same routes in spring and autumn.

14

FOSSIL HAWKS
AND OWLS

Because birds have wings and can fly, and have very fragile bones which are hollow, they normally do not become trapped in a situation which leads to their fossilization. Hence the fossil record of birds is known far less perfectly than that of other classes of vertebrates such as reptiles and mammals. Still, some remarkable fossil birds have been discovered and this has given us important insights into the evolution of hawks and owls.

Of course, nobody knows exactly when the first recognizable bird actually appeared. The first *known* bird lived about 130 million years ago, during the Upper Jurassic period in Bavaria. Scientists named the bird *Archaeopteryx lithographica*. meaning ancient wing preserved in stone. It was an amazing creature. In many ways it strongly resembled a reptile. But, more important, it clearly showed that birds evolved from primitive, unspecialized thecodont reptiles. Like modern birds, *Archaeopteryx* shared many skeletal features common with reptiles, but it also was covered with feathers. (By definition, any animal with feathers is a bird.) However, the arrangement of some of the feathers (particularly on the tail) differed considerably from the arrangement of tail feathers on modern birds. Nonetheless, recent studies show that the basic structure of the ancient feathers differed in no significant way from that of modern birds. Indeed, it is ironical that the fossil record of *Archaeopteryx* is so amazingly complete and detailed that we know far more about it than about many more recent fossil birds.

Unfortunately, the fossil record of hawks and owls is poorly known. Some species appear in the Eocene record about 60 million years ago. During this epoch, the ancestors of our modern typical owls appeared in Wyoming. But of all the North American species of this period, the Stilt Vulture *(Neocathartes grallator)* probably is the most interesting. It also was found in Wyoming. Its long legs and well-developed toes, but reduced wings, suggest that it could fly although it probably was basically terrestrial. No doubt it was a scavenger. But it was so distinct that paleontologist Hildegarde Howard points out that it represents a distinct family of American vultures—a family which disappeared from the fossil record after the Eocene epoch.

Paleontologists are faced with many difficult and unsolved puzzles when they study the evolution and distribution of fossil vultures. For example, the Cathartid or American vultures once were distributed in North America as well as in Europe. Indeed, they appear in the European fossil record during the Middle Eocene, but do not occur in North American fossil deposits until the Lower Oligocene. American vultures then disappeared from Europe, but continued to survive in the New World during the Oligocene. However, a different group, the Old World vultures, also appeared during the Miocene from Europe and North America. These birds lived on both continents for millions of years, then became extinct in the New World in postglacial times.

Hawks, eagles, falcons, and owls seem to be somewhat more recent than the oldest vultures. The buteos, or soaring hawks, for example, make their first fossil appearance during the Upper Oligocene and Miocene epochs. Related to living species such as the Red-tailed and Broad-winged Hawks, the fossil birds were somewhat larger in size than living species. Eagles of the genus *Aquila,* of which the Golden Eagle is an example, also appear in fossil deposits during the Oligocene epoch of Europe and North America. They had larger feet with longer and more powerful toes, but otherwise they appear to have been less powerful soaring birds in comparison with modern eagles. Eared or tufted owls of the genus *Asio* and the considerably larger and more powerful horned owls of the genus *Bubo* also appeared during the Oligocene epoch.

During the Miocene a large variety of raptors appeared. Included were sea eagles of the genus *Haliaeetus,* of which our Bald Eagle is a representative, along with true falcons, Barn Owls, owls of the genus *Strix,* and many other birds of prey. And, by the time the Pleistocene epoch began one million years ago, the harriers, the accipitrine or forest dwelling hawks, the fish-eating Ospreys, and the *Otus* and *Glaucidium* owls all had evolved.

Three particularly important bird-bearing fossil deposits, 149 unusually rich in predatory birds, occur in California. The most famous of these, the asphalt deposits at Rancho La Brea in Los Angeles, contains fossils of birds which lived in a woodland whose vegetation was composed of light-growth brush and trees. The second site, known as the McKittrick deposit, is located in the southern San Joaquin Valley. The birds preserved here lived in a marsh or perhaps around a small desert lake. Finally, the third deposit, known as the Carpinteria beds, is located on cliffs along the ocean north of Ventura. The birds preserved here probably lived in coastal forest.

The asphalt or tar pools at Rancho La Brea, in particular, were extremely efficient natural traps which held virtually any animal touching the sticky material. Once an animal became mired, others (particularly predatory birds and mammals) were attracted to the stricken creature's struggles and cries. But the prospect of an easy feast turned into a trap for these predators, too, and they also were trapped and eventually were fossilized.

The resulting fossil deposits do not occur in a single spot, however. According to Hildegarde Howard, one of the paleontologists who excavated many of the specimens at this site,

> the tar seeps extended over a space of 23 acres, and fossils were removed from twenty separate deposits. The combined collections from these several pits at Rancho La Brea have provided an unusually full record for this area. In no single deposit, however, were all the listed species found. Even in the pit yielding the most abundant avian remains (from which at least 30,000 bones were recovered), only 81 of the 113 species were present. Possibly the traps were active at different times within the Ice Age, but, on the other hand, immediate ecologic conditions no doubt played an important part. . . . The rare Daggett Eagle occurred in only two pits, a curious fact which may be associated with geologic age, but could also be explained by the presence of a favorite type of plant growth.

Two-thirds of the birds recovered at Rancho La Brea were birds of prey. Among the most spectacular and impressive creatures was a condor-like vulture named *Teratornis merriami*. This bird had a wingspread reaching at least 12 feet, it stood some two and one-half feet high, and weighed 40 or 50 pounds. In short, it was one of the largest known flying birds. It also occurred in Pleistocene deposits in Mexico and Florida. But even more impressive is *Teratornis incredibilis,* a condor-like vulture recovered from other Pleistocene deposits in Nevada and late Pliocene deposits in California. This gigantic creature had bones roughly 40 percent larger than *Teratornis merriami,* suggesting that it might have had a wingspread of 16 or 17 feet! The endangered and nearly extinct

California Condor, with a wingspread reaching a maximum of about 9 and one-half feet, is dwarfed in comparison.

Curiously, the California Condor is well represented in the Rancho La Brea fossil deposits. This indicates that it once was relatively common in California.

Two additional species of condors occurred in these deposits. The rare Brea Condor *(Breagyps clarki)* had the proportions of the Black Vulture, but was much larger, with a very long and slender bill. In contrast, *Gymnogyps amplus* was a very abundant species which closely resembled the nearly extinct California Condor.

Two smaller vultures also appear in the Rancho La Brea deposits. Turkey Vultures, for example, apparently were rare during the Pleistocene, judging from the small number of skeletons recovered, but have greatly increased in numbers during the past 50 thousand years. On the other hand, the extinct Occidental Vulture *(Coragyps occidentalis)* was a common bird. This species also has been found in sites in Nevada, New Mexico, and Mexico.

Several small scavengers also occurred at Rancho La Brea. The American Neophron *(Neophrontops americanus)* was related to the Old World vultures, particularly to the Egyptian Vulture *(Neophron percnopterus)* which still lives in Africa and parts of Europe. It would be fascinating to know if the American Neophron learned to fling stones at birds' eggs to break them (thus exhibiting true tool-using behavior) as some Egyptian Vultures in East Africa do when they discover Ostrich eggs.

The La Brea Caracara *(Polyborus prelutosus)*, a 12-inch-high bird, was the other small scavenger. Its bones closely resembled those of the recently extinct Guadalupe Caracara discussed in chapter 7. Hildegarde Howard suggests that it may represent the ancestral stock from which the living caracara species evolved.

In addition to the birds already discussed, eagles of a variety of species were especially common at Rancho La Brea. At least seven species occurred there. Two of these still survive—the Golden Eagle and the Bald Eagle.

The largest of the extinct eagles, and one unique to this site, is known as the Woodward Eagle *(Morphnus woodwardi)*. Because of it's long and heavy leg bones, and powerful body and wings, it is perhaps related to the powerful Harpy Eagles of South America. Another rare species, the Daggett Eagle *(Wetmoregyps daggetti)*, had exceptionally long, slender legs. At a glance at a drawing, it suggests the Secretary Bird of Africa, but upon careful study of the limited fossil remains it appears the bird may show a closer relationship with certain long-legged South American hawks.

Of the three smaller eagles represented in abundance in the fossil record, the Errant Eagle *(Neogyps errans)* was related to the

Old World vultures (which are degenerate eagles). However, the New World branch of this group was separated from the Old World birds for a very long period of time. In any event, the bird was roughly the size of the Golden Eagle but it had shorter legs and longer wing bones. The Grinnell Eagle *(Spizaetus grinnelli)*, on the other hand, was more closely related to the spectacular crested eagles still living in Central and South America, and the Fragile Eagle *(Buteogallus fragilis)*, a bird of quite slender proportions, seems most closely related to the Black Hawk now found in tropical and sub-tropical America and as far north as the southwestern United States.

In addition to those diurnal raptors which are extinct, a number of species still living also occurred at Rancho La Brea: Turkey Vultures, California Condors, White-tailed Kites, Northern Goshawks, Sharp-shinned Hawks, Cooper's Hawks, Red-tailed Hawks, Red-shouldered Hawks (?), Swainson's Hawks, Rough-legged Hawks, Golden Eagles, Bald Eagles, Prairie Falcons, Peregrine Falcons, Merlins, and American Kestrels. At the McKittrick site in California, another very large extinct falcon also occurred. It is named the Swarth Falcon *(Falco swarthi)*.

Owls also lived at Rancho La Brea, and all species except one still are alive. The Brea Owl *(Strix brea)* is extinct. It was larger than its living relatives, Barred and Spotted Owls. Among the species still living, Great Horned Owls were abundant, and Barn Owls were somewhat less numerous. Burrowing Owls were still less common, and small species such as the Screech, Pygmy, and Saw-whet Owls apparently were very rare judging from the few specimens recovered.

This chapter does not cover all fossil birds of prey known from North America (some are poorly preserved and their status uncertain), but it does illustrate that constant changes took place in raptor species and populations throughout vast periods of geologic time. The highlights of some of these changes, involved with the evolution of our birds of prey, are preserved and revealed to us in the fossil record.

15

ENDANGERED RAPTORS

The changes which occurred in species and populations of fossil hawks and owls were not only phenomena of the past. Because of their ecological roles as predators, most birds of prey have suffered greatly at the hands of man during the past century. Egg collecting, shooting, poisoning, pole trapping (with traps set on tall poles), habitat destruction, and more recently pesticides and falconry all have combined to reduce the numbers of hawks and owls surviving in the wild. As a result, some North American birds of prey now are either on the brink of extinction or severely reduced in numbers. In either case they are recognized as endangered species by the United States Fish and Wildlife Service. These are species or subspecies that are so rare now that their prospects for survival and reproduction are in immediate jeopardy. Extinction probably will follow unless they receive immediate and effective help. In the continental United States, the following birds of prey currently are endangered species: California Condor, Snail (Everglade) Kite, Bald Eagle, and Peregrine Falcon. In addition a number of other species also are seriously reduced in numbers but are not yet considered endangered species.

At least three major reasons can be cited for the current endangered status of these four species: shooting, habitat destruction, and pesticide pollution.　　153

Shooting

Although intensive hawk shooting campaigns such as occurred earlier in this century in New Jersey and Pennsylvania no longer occur, widespread random shooting of birds of prey still continues throughout the country. Far too many hunters still can't resist taking a shot at a hawk or owl. This problem, however, is not restricted entirely to North America. Many raptors from North America are shot as they migrate through, or winter in, the West Indies or Central and South America. In Europe the situation is just as bad. Maarten Bijleveld, in *Birds of Prey in Europe*, documents a disastrous reduction of raptor populations there due to shooting and trapping during the past century or more. Only within recent years have Europeans shown increased concern about the welfare of birds of prey and taken the necessary steps to provide these birds with legal protection.

One of the most alarming recent examples of illegal shooting of raptors in North America occurred (and still does) in the Southwest. Sheep ranchers, many of whom use public lands on which they graze their livestock, hired helicopter and airplane pilots to kill as many eagles as possible from the air. In 1971, for example, over 700 Golden Eagles and some Bald Eagles were shot by pilots working for several ranchers in Wyoming and Colorado. The birds were fully protected by federal statute at the time they were shot. Prior to these incidents, aerial shooting of eagles long had been done by ranchers in the Trans-Pecos and Edwards Plateau sections of Texas. Over the years, thousands of eagles have been killed because of such illegal activities.

In addition to such organized hawk shooting efforts, some hunters and ranchers in the West occasionally shoot hawks perched along roads passing through deserts, prairies, ranchland, and other areas. Even endangered species such as the California Condor are not immune from gunners. Despite the widespread publicity given condors in recent years, wanton shooting still results in the loss of some birds. One man stated he wanted to shoot a condor simply to see what the bird looked like! Another threatened to shoot every condor he could to end the condor problem once and for all! In the case of a species as rare as the California Condor, where 40 or fewer birds survive, shooting can be a major factor in hastening the extinction of the species. Every possible effort, therefore, must be made to try to inform and educate hunters about the plight of condors, their appearance, and especially the fact that they are fully protected birds.

Some hunters also shoot endangered Peregrine Falcons. In a recent case in New Jersey, a bird reared in captivity at Cornell

University and later released into the wild as part of a Peregrine management program was shot. The bird was fitted with a tiny radio transmitter which may have attracted the attention of the hunter who became curious. The man responsible for the shooting was eventually arrested and severely fined.

The ecological damage which shooting of eagles and other birds of prey inflicts upon food chains and food webs often far removed from the locations where the birds are shot seldom is considered. Most of these birds, particularly eagles, require large geographic areas for nesting and hunting. Therefore, when they are shot, or otherwise removed from the environment, portions of raptor populations from large geographic areas are eliminated and thus prevented from carrying out necessary roles in helping to maintain the balance of nature. Sometimes shooting depletes birds of prey from thousands of square miles of land. It is difficult to determine all of the long range effects which shooting has on the ecology of entire regions, but sometimes some short range effects such as marked increases in the numbers of rodents or rabbits are noted. In severe situations the whole composition of an area's vegetation can be altered. In turn, this can lead to major changes in the species of wildlife living in such areas.

Habitat Destruction

The major importance of habitat to the survival of wildlife (and plantlife) cannot be overemphasized. Yet habitat destruction is second only to pesticides as a major force leading to the marked decline in the numbers of many birds of prey in North America in recent years. Although habitat destruction was less important than pesticides in the decline of the Peregrine Falcon, it combined with pesticide pollution to become a major cause of the decline of the Bald Eagle in the lower 48 states.

A case in point is famous Mount Johnson Island in the Susquehanna River near Lancaster, Pennsylvania. During the 1930's and 1940's the island supported a large and impressive Bald Eagle nest. In 1935, Herbert H. Beck, a noted ornithologist and naturalist from Franklin and Marshall College, took several well know conservationists to the island to inspect the eagle nest. One of the visitors, Richard H. Pough, recognized the conservation importance of Mount Johnson Island and arranged to lease the island for the National Audubon Society. Thus was created the world's first eagle sanctuary. Professor Beck was appointed the custodian of the sanctuary. Later, when Beck retired, Theodore R. Hake was appointed Audubon wildlife warden in charge of the sanctuary.

Over the years the eagles of Mount Johnson Island have successfully raised at least 22 eaglets despite several disasters during which the nest was blown from its supporting tree. However, between 1948 and 1960, no eagles nested successfully despite the presence of the adults birds on the island. The causes for the reproductive failures are not known, but pesticides almost certainly were responsible. In any event, in 1959 the owners of the island, a local electric power company, announced plans to construct electric power lines there. Thus habitat destruction, coupled with pesticide pollution, ruined one of the most historic Bald Eagle nests in the United States. Similar loss of eagle habitat (not due to power line construction) led to the abandonment of the famous Bald Eagle nest at Vermillion, Ohio. The nest was blown down during a storm.

Recent conservation efforts on behalf of the Bald Eagle by the National Wildlife Federation, The Nature Conservancy, and other noted wildlife conservation organizations have resulted in the saving of several major Bald Eagle winter roosts. Some were presented to the federal government and now are being maintained as special national wildlife refuges.

The endangered Snail Kite, known in Florida as the Everglade Kite, provides another example of how habitat destruction or change can seriously threaten the survival of endangered forms of wildlife. In the United States, this species is restricted to southern Florida where it requires freshwater marshes which support adequate quantitites of a snail named *Pomacea paludosa*. The mollusk is the primary food eaten by Snail Kites.

Unfortunately the destruction by "development" of the vast freshwater marshes which once existed in southern Florida has contributed directly to the reduction of the kite's geographic range and to its dwindling numbers, now down to only a few dozen. Many areas once were used regularly as breeding grounds by the kites, but with marsh conversion to agricultural areas where citrus is grown and cattle is grazed, plus the development of complicated flood and water control facilities, the kites have abandoned such areas. Flood control facilities also are serious negative ecological factors threatening kite survival during recent years. In their report on the current status of the kite, Walter O. Stieglitz and Richard L. Thompson state: "Adequate water levels are the key to kite use of any area. Unless a permanent water supply can be maintained to support populations and the proper vegetative complex the area will become valueless to the birds." They also state that current knowledge of the life history of the snail forming the kite's sole food supply is too inadequate to evelute fully the effects of low water levels upon molluscan populations. Nevertheless, prolonged dry periods are known to damage aquatic molluscan populations. Hence, if vital water supplies are diverted from freshwater marshes being utilized by Snail Kites, the birds eventually will disappear

The survival of the Snail Kite in Florida depends upon the protection and preservation of freshwater marshes in which Pomacea snails live in adequate numbers to provide food for the kites. Photo by Donald Pfitzer/U.S. Fish and Wildlife Service.

because of a serious depletion of their specialized food supply. Should that happen, the birds will become extinct since they are incapable of resorting to another type of food.

California Condors also have suffered greatly from habitat loss and destruction as well as inadequate reproduction. As a result only about 40 condors still survive in California, and the survival of the species remains extremely precarious.

Organized scientific efforts are under way, however, to try to save the California Condor and other endangered species. Federal officials have prepared "recovery plans" for each species, including the condors, and teams of biologists currently are hard at work putting the plans into action. The idea upon which a recovery plan is based is clear, as explained in the California Condor Recovery Plan:

> With some species of animals in the United States in immediate danger of becoming extinct, orderly approaches to preservation are 157

An immature California Condor. Unless many more young condors are raised this species will become extinct. Photo by Sanford R. Wilbur/U.S. Fish and Wildlife Service.

mandatory. We do not have the time to experiment with piecemeal approaches or partial solutions: we have to attack the total problem. The Recovery Plan serves as a guide for such efforts. Prepared by a group of biologists and other individuals most knowledgeable of a species and its needs, the Plan is a formal presentation of the problem, setting management goals, and providing a list of necessary actions and a timetable for completing them. For some species whose needs are well known and management efforts are relatively simple, a recovery plan may be brief and easily implemented. Others with complex ecological problems may require a major cooperative effort. For most species, the goal for preservation is complete recovery—return of the population to a nonendangered status. For a few, we may only be able to hold the line against further loss of habitat or numbers.

The goals of the California Condor Recovery Plan are equally specific: "To maintain a minimum population of at least 50 California Condors, well distributed throughout their 1974 base range with an average natality (birth rate) of at least 4 young per year, and the lowest possible annual mortality." To achieve this goal, at least four vital actions must be carried out.

158

1. Adequate nesting conditions will be provided for the condors.
2. Adequate roosting sites also will be provided.
3. Adequate food will be provided.
4. Rigid protection will be given to the birds.

In addition, a program of captive breeding of condors will be undertaken, the ultimate objective being the eventual return into the wild of the birds raised in captivity.

Pesticides

One of man's most controversial environmental activities is the widespread use of pesticides in the biosphere. Although some pesticides such as DDT now are banned from use in the United States, Canada, and various European countries, DDT and its relatives still are used widely and in large quantities in Latin America where various migratory birds of prey from North America are exposed to the chemicals. DDT and dieldrin, in particular, have become two of the most dangerous, troublesome, and persistent environmental pollutants. They have contaminated virtually all animal life ranging from tiny creatures in the deepest ocean trenches and most remote corners of the globe to man himself. Today much is known about the undesirable effects of DDT upon animals, particularly birds, but some of the complex story still is being uncovered by ecologists and wildlife biologists. Current knowledge, however, clearly demonstrates that the widespread and continued use of these pesticides in areas outside of the United States still represents an environmental disaster of the most serious sort.

Birds of prey, in particular, have suffered from the sublethal effects of DDT and its common metabolite DDE. Evidence also indicates that dieldrin is sometimes responsible for serious undesirable effects upon many birds of prey. The story of the disastrous sublethal effects of DDT on the Peregrine Falcon (and Bald Eagle) most vividly illustrates the role which this pesticide plays in cycling throughout the environment, in contaminating food chains and food webs, and in dramatically altering the reproductive physiology and biology of an increasingly numerous variety of birds.

For centuries the Peregrine Falcon has been admired as one of the most perfectly evolved species in the world. It is distributed nearly worldwide; three subspecies are found in North America. However, Peregrines never were abundant throughout their range. According to Roger Tory Peterson, probably no more than 5,000 individuals originally populated the entire North American continent. Because of the Peregrine's position at the top of a food chain, a continental population of this limited size would be expected and is normal. In 1942, a survey of Peregrine nesting eyries east of the Rocky Mountains revealed the existence of 408 sites. Joseph J. Hickey, the biologist conducting the survey, estimated that an 11 percent decline had occurred from the original population level estimated in this area.

Today the Peregrine Falcon is extirpated as a breeding bird in most of North America south of Alaska and Canada although a few pairs still nest successfully in the West.

The story of the extirpation of this falcon as a breeding bird began with the unrestricted and widespread spraying of DDT into the environment soon after the end of the Second World War. Considerable quantities of the pesticide were used in the United States, in Great Britain, and throughout Europe. With continued use, increasingly large quantities of the long-lived chemical entered food chains and food webs on a worldwide scale. Particularly large quantities were detected in Britain, Europe, and the United States. Passed link by link, from animal to animal, throughout food chains and webs, the extremely fat-soluble DDT increased to alarming concentrations in the fat of many animals—especially birds of prey. In addition to the pesticide's tendency to concentrate in fatty tissues of animals, it also becomes magnified (increased in quantity and concentration) each time it is passed to the next higher link in a food chain. Thus birds such as Peregrines, Bald Eagles, and various other raptors, which occupy ecological positions at the tops of food chains, accumulate the original quantities of DDT residues plus all of the extra residues which animals lower in the food chain store in their fatty tissues for varying periods of time.

With huge quantitites of pesticides stored in their fat, strange events occurred as the Peregrines began their breeding cycles. The falcons' eggs broke unusually easy. The birds ate the contents of their own eggs. This pathological behavior first was noted in eyries in Massachusetts in 1947, was repeated in Quebec eyries in 1949, and in Pennsylvania eyries in 1949 and 1950. Similar behavior occurred in 1951 in Peregrine eyries in Great Britain. By 1962, pathological behavior became widespread in Northern Hemisphere Peregrine populations, and the birds suffered severe population crashes in the United States, Great Britain, France, Germany, Finland, Sweden, Switzerland, Ireland, and Belgium, and a slight decline in Norway.

Wildlife biologists recognized that a variety of causes could have been responsible for the strange behavior and failure of nesting efforts. Many possibilities were considered. But pesticides such as DDT seemed the most likely cause. The population crashes correlated closely with geographic and temporal uses of organochlorine pesticides in the environment. Intensive research into the problem continued in Great Britain and in America. By 1969, investigators demonstrated that DDE (one of DDT's common metabolite or breakdown products) induces liver enzymes in birds which inactivate certain sex hormones, notably estrogen. This was an important discovery. Estrogen is closely involved in calcium chemistry in birds. Thus, as DDT levels increased in birds of prey such as Peregrines, the pesticide was metabolized into DDE, calcium ATPase activity was altered, and the birds laid eggs with unusually thin shells which tended to break easily as the birds incubated them. Once the eggs were broken, the calcium-starved falcons instinctively ate their own eggs! This resulted in widespread Peregrine nesting failures throughout much of the Northern Hemisphere, and the falcons have been brought nearly to the brink of extinction in many areas.

But federal wildlife biologists wanted still more conclusive evidence demonstrating that DDT caused the thin eggshell syndrome in predatory birds. Investigators at the United States Department of the Interior's Patuxent Wildlife Research Center at Laurel, Maryland, conducted controlled experiments in which Mallards and American Kestrels were fed measured quantities of DDT mixed with their food—quantities approximating residue levels then found in nature. The results were significant. The birds exhibited marked thinning of eggshells, some embryos of ducks died, and the patterns of reproductive failure of both species closely corresponded to the Peregrine's reproductive failure.

Equally important, a continuous program of monitoring eggshell thickness and reproductive success of a variety of North American birds demonstrated that thin eggshells and lowered reproductuve success appeared in an alarming number of birds of prey including the Bald Eagle. Moreover, a large number of nonpredatory birds also produced thin eggshells. The West Coast population of the Brown Pelican, for example, had nearly a 100 percent reproductive failure due to DDT pollution. Other birds also produced eggs with unusually thin shells: herons and egrets, cormorants, gulls, and murres. Most of the affected species more or less are associated with wetlands and aquatic habitats.

In Pennsylvania, where the extirpation of the Peregrine Falcon (as a breeding bird) is total, 34 eyries once were occupied. Bald Eagles nested in considerable numbers through the lower 48 states until after World War II. They, too, have been completely eliminated as nesting birds in many areas and have been seriously reduced in numbers elsewhere. In New Jersey, for example, there are no Bald Eagles now nesting successfully although, in the past, a

dozen or more eagle nests were productive in that state. Only in Alaska, where the large northern subspecies of the Bald Eagle lives, is the national bird of the United States still common.

Recently, however, some Bald Eagles and other birds of prey seem to be showing a welcome recovery in breeding success in some portions of the lower 48 states. This apparently is happening because DDT and other organochlorine pesticides now are banned from use within the United States and they are therefore slowly being eliminated from natural ecosystems. Thus the birds of prey seem to be responding favorably to a cleaner environment as far as these chemicals are concerned.

Unfortunately the Peregrine Falcon population in North America was so seriously reduced in numbers that elaborate captive breeding programs now are being used to produce young Peregrines for reintroduction into the wild in parts of their former nesting range. Some of these captive-reared birds now are living in the wild and there seems to be hope that they will reuse some of the former eyries, and other sites, and begin to nest successfully as natural members of the wildlife community. However, some years will have to pass before the effectiveness of the program can be fully evaluated. Nevertheless, hope has returned for the Peregrine Falcon, Bald Eagle, and various other birds of prey.

A captive Peregrine Falcon used for endangered species research at the Patuxent Wildlife Research Center, Laurel, Maryland. Photo by Luther C. Goldman/U.S. Fish and Wildlife Service.

16

INCREASING RAPTOR POPULATIONS

Although most hawks, and some owls, have declined in numbers during this century, a few species have reacted favorably to changing environmental conditions. These species are in the minority, however, and wildlife biologists are uncertain if these trends will continue or if they are short term reactions to environmental changes.

Natural Changes

The history of evolution of life is one of constant change, experimentation, and adaption or lack of it. We need only consider the giant tree ferns which once abounded in Pennsylvania, but which died out and are preserved as that state's great coal beds, or the dinosaurs which roamed widely throughout North America, then became extinct millions of years ago, to appreciate how changing environmental conditions profoundly affect animals and plants. Birds of prey equally are influenced by changes in the environment.

The Black Vulture is one of the species which seems to be reacting favorably to undetermined environmental changes. At a time when many birds of prey are declining rapidly in numbers, this vulture is expanding its breeding range northward. Formerly Black Vultures were restricted to the warmer southern portions of the

United States, Central and South America, and Trinidad. At best, they were casual visitors in the northern half of the United States. But within recent years, Black Vultures have appeared with increasing frequency in northern states. The birds now breed in south central Pennsylvania where previously they never did.

Over the past few decades there also has been a slow northward expansion of the breeding range of the Turkey Vulture. Likewise, the Barn Owl also is extending its breeding range into northern areas where it previously never had been known.

Habitat Changes

Man's drastic changes in the environment occasionally have beneficial effects upon some species of wildlife. When a forest is cleared to create a field, for example, different birds and other wildlife enter and become established. The American Kestrel is one species which is responding favorably to the opening of fields and agricultural regions. The kestrels are increasing in numbers, apparently because there is more habitat available in which to nest and feed.

In addition, many conservation organizations and some interested individuals are putting nest boxes in suitable spots in an effort to attract kestrels to use them as nests. The results are remarkable. The falcons readily accept them, and substantial kestrel populations have been developed in some areas. Thus far they have not been affected by the thin eggshell problem which has destroyed the reproductive capacity of larger falcons such as Peregrines. But kestrels occupy a lower feeding level in the ecosystem, and it probably will take longer for such effects to become obvious.

In California, White-tailed Kites have increased in numbers during recent years. Current agricultural practices now allow the birds to utilize more open country and cultivated bottomlands than in the past.

The Screech Owl also provides an example of a raptor which may be increasing in numbers. It occupies an ecological niche similar to that occupied by the American Kestrel, except that it is nocturnal in behavior. Hence the kestrels and the owls complement each other in habitat and niche requirements. In fact, the two species frequently use the same types of nest sites. Not infrequently, Screech Owls roost and even nest in boxes put out for kestrels. They also are known to nest in boxes put out for Wood Ducks in marshes. To this extent, the Screech Owl's habitat requirements vary somewhat from those of the kestrel.

165

17

RAPTOR CONSERVATION EFFORTS

Despite the many serious problems faced by various North American raptors, a considerable variety of conservation and management techniques is being developed and used by raptor conservationists and biologists to aid these birds. It is worthwhile, therefore, to discuss some of the most important of these efforts in this chapter.

Special Refuges and Natural Areas

Because preservation of raptor habitat is vital to the survival of these birds, increased emphasis now is being placed on obtaining exceptionally important raptor migration, breeding, and wintering natural areas. In some instances, federal or state governments are responsible for the purchase of such sites, but frequently private conservation organizations and/or groups of private individuals take the necessary action to acquire the sites. In a few instances, corporations have cooperated with concerned persons in order to establish special raptor refuges. Far more can be done within the United States and Canada to establish such refuges or natural areas, however, and it is hoped that this section of the book will interest more people in working toward creating such sites in many parts of both countries. The following examples illustrate the variety of facilities that can be developed provided they are based upon sound biological and ecological information.

A hawk's eye (aerial) view of the North Lookout at Hawk Mountain Sanctuary, Pennsylvania. In 1934 bird watchers purchased the mountain to stop the shooting of migrating hawks at that site and thus established a precedent in North America for the creation of special wildlife refuges for birds of prey.

Migration Areas

Hawk Mountain Sanctuary in eastern Pennsylvania was the first refuge for birds of prey in the world. It was established in 1934 by a group of concerned individuals to stop the shooting of thousands of migrating hawks passing that spot in autumn. Today thousands of people visit Hawk Mountain to observe and photograph the birds instead of to shoot them. In a similar manner, most of the former hawk shooting sites elsewhere in the vicinity of Hawk Mountain also now are popular hawk watching lookouts. Indeed the Pennsylvania Game Commission recently designated the entire length of the Kittatinny Ridge in southeastern Pennsylvania as the Kittatinny Ridge Birds of Prey Natural Area. The section

Maurice Broun, in 1956, on the lookout at Hawk Mountain Sanctuary, Pennsylvania. Broun was the first curator of Hawk Mountain and was responsible for turning a hawk slaughter ground into a world famous wildlife sanctuary.

involved runs from the Delaware Water Gap west to Waggoner's Gap just north of Carlisle. Similarly the well-known hawk lookouts located on the Lehigh County section of the same ridge were recognized and designated as the Lehigh County Raptor Migration Area by an official resolution issued by the Lehigh County executive. Thus the exceptional scientific and conservation-education significance of Pennsylvania's hawk lookouts is recognized by the state and county and called to the public's attention.

Some hawk lookouts in other states also are protected and operated as special raptor refuges. In New Jersey, for example, the Montclair Hawk Lookout Sanctuary is owned and operated by the

168

Cedar Island is owned by the State of New Jersey and maintained as a special Osprey nesting refuge.

New Jersey Audubon Society whereas the famous hawk lookout at Cape May Point now is a state park. Similarly, in Minnesota, the Hawk Ridge Nature Reserve is operated by the Duluth Audubon Society. It is one of the most important hawk migration lookouts in the Great Lakes Region.

Breeding Areas

Several important raptor breeding areas also are now protected as refuges for birds of prey. In New Jersey, for example, Cedar Island was purchased by the state as an Osprey nesting refuge. In Idaho the federal government established the Snake River Birds of Prey Natural Area on lands owned by the

A nestling Osprey on Cedar Island, New Jersey.

169

Department of the Interior. Here protection is provided for what may be the most dense population of nesting birds of prey in North America. Golden Eagles and Prairie Falcons are particularly numerous and various other species also use the area during the breeding season or at other times of the year.

Wintering Areas

A variety of wintering areas, many used by Bald Eagles, also are established as special refuges for raptors. In Wisconsin, for instance, a group of individuals forming the Eagle Valley Environmentalists, Inc., own and protect several sites used by Bald Eagles during winter. In Washington the state government established the Skagit River Bald Eagle Natural Area in cooperation with The Nature Conservancy, and in California the Hunt-Wesson Hawk and Owl Preserve was established through the cooperation of some local Audubon members and officials of Hunt-Wesson Foods, Inc.

The establishment of other raptor refuges in various parts of the United States resulted from the efforts of various private individuals, government agencies, and other organizations. Those discussed provide a brief picture of what can be done to help save various types of habitats needed by birds of prey.

Traps

In years past, game managers, operators of game farms, and other persons frequently used pole traps (steel-jawed traps placed on top of tall poles) to capture hawks and owls and thus remove them from wildlife management areas used for hunting, shooting preserves, and similar facilities. Because birds of prey naturally tend to land on tall perches such as poles, the birds were easily captured in the traps and either were killed outright or, more frequently, suffered broken legs or other broken bones and slow, lingering deaths. Sometimes the birds were not removed from the traps for days or even weeks after being caught. Pole traps were both inhumane and indiscriminate in what they caught. Countless raptors were destroyed over the years in these brutal devices. Concerned citizens therefore demanded that they be outlawed and they are rarely used today in most areas.

When an occasional troublesome hawk or owl now visits an area and must be removed for one reason or another, the birds can be trapped alive in a safe and humane manner with a modified and improved version of the Swedish Goshawk trap developed by Heinz Meng. The captured birds then can be transported to other

170

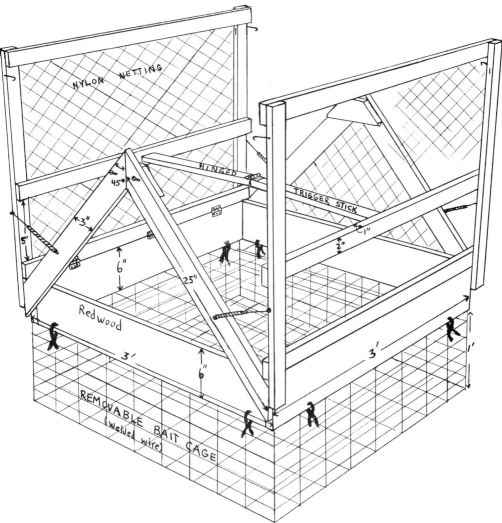

The redesigned, modified, and improved Swedish Goshawk trap developed by Heinz Meng. From Meng (1971) in the Journal of Wildlife Management.

areas and released alive in a suitable habitat. Sometimes a variety of other devices also are used to capture birds of prey, but in all instances such captures must be made by qualified persons under authority of state and federal permits. State and federal wildlife authorities can provide full details upon request.

171

Artificial Nest Structures

Another excellent way in which conservationists can aid certain species of birds of prey is by building artificial nest structures. For example, Turkey Vultures sometimes can be induced to use special boxes or shelters as nesting sites if they are placed in wooded areas in locations where vultures are common. Great Horned Owls also sometimes accept as the foundation for their nest old rubber tires placed securely in the fork or crotch of a tall tree in wooded areas. The owls then add sticks and other materials to the tire foundation and carry out their nesting cycle.

American Kestrels and Screech Owls, however, are the best known examples of North American birds of prey which readily accept nest boxes as substitutes for natural tree cavities in which to nest. Thus the construction and placement of these boxes in suitable habitats (often open agricultural areas) can effectively maintain or even increase the breeding populations of the falcons and/or owls. Both American Kestrels and Screech Owls accept the same size box. The essential dimensions are 11 inches deep, 11 inches wide, and 12 inches high. An entrance opening at the top of the front of the box should measure about 3 inches wide and 4 inches high and the bottom of the corners of the opening should be rounded. A few drainage holes can be bored into the bottom of the box, and a small space between the top and the side will allow for ventilation. In addition, a small perch *inside* the box just below the entrance opening will allow the nestlings to look out. About 3 inches of shavings or sawdust should be placed on the bottom of the box to provide a safer place for the female to lay her eggs. The boxes need not be cleaned every year, but many conservationists do clean them to prolong the life of the boxes and to remove debris which other birds or animals occasionally place in the boxes after the American Kestrels or Screech Owls have finished nesting. These birds also will sometimes accept old wooden barrels, with an entrance hole cut into the front, as nest sites if they are placed 20 feet or higher in trees. Generally the boxes or barrels should be fastened in place with the entrance opening facing south.

Artificial Feeding Stations

In a few instances, certain birds of prey can be provided with food by putting it at suitable locations where the birds will find it and learn to return regularly. For example, carcasses of domestic livestock or road-killed deer or other wild animals sometimes are put in open areas for the use of Turkey Vultures and Black Vultures. Similarly, in California, some artificial feeding programs have been carried out for California Condors. In New Jersey one conservationist built a large tank and stocked it with live fish for the benefit of Ospreys in the area. Such artificial feeding stations can provide valuable supplemental food supplies for these birds when natural food supplies are unavailable or inadequate.

Nest Wardening

Nest wardening is used primarily at rare raptor nests in Britain and Europe, but a limited number of wardening efforts also have been attempted in the United States. The technique usually involves a number of persons, often volunteers, who maintain a continuous around-the-clock guard of the nests from a safe distance. The purpose of such intensive efforts is to prevent falconers or egg collectors from robbing nestlings or eggs from the nests, or photographers from disturbing the nests. Wardening also puts considerable emphasis on developing good public relations for the birds involved so that eventually such costly and intensive efforts may not have to be used.

Perhaps the most notable recent example of nest wardening in the United States took place at the famous Peregrine Falcon eyrie on Moro Rock in California. An elaborate network of wardens, aided by sophisticated and costly electronic equipment, was used to prevent falconers from stealing the nestlings. In the future, however, as more captive-reared endangered species are placed back into the wild, it is likely that more nest wardening will become necessary to assure the birds' safety and survival.

Raptor Rehabilitation

In recent years various persons have begun to rehabilitate birds of prey with broken wings or other injuries and have released them back into the wild when possible. Such efforts receive considerable publicity in the news media but are most worthwhile when injured endangered species are involved. Some raptor biologists feel that the time spent working with injured raptors which are very common could be used better and more productively in other aspects of raptor conservation such as construction of artificial nest structures, preservation of vital habitat, or related areas of concern. However, when time and funds are available to devote attention to all aspects of raptor conservation, efforts to salvage common species also can be rewarding and worthwhile.

Captive Breeding and Reintroduction

The breeding of Peregrine Falcons and other endangered birds of prey in captivity, with the ultimate objective of reintroducing the captive-reared birds into the wild and having them establish themselves as wild breeding birds, is a new raptor conservation effort. Although Peregrine Falcons were bred in captivity successfully in the early 1940's in Germany, Heinz Meng was the first American to duplicate that achievement in the United States in 1970 and 1971. Today he continues his Peregrine breeding efforts with increased success in new facilities at the New Paltz Peregrine Falcon Foundation, Inc., at New Paltz, New York.

A similar but much larger and more ambitious program has been in progress since 1973 at Cornell University's Laboratory of Ornithology under the direction of Tom Cade. The Cornell program has now produced enough captive-reared Peregrines to begin reintroducing some birds into the wild at various carefully selected locations. The results thus far, however, have not been without problems. One bird was shot in New Jersey by a hunter, and other birds died from a fungus disease acquired while still in captivity. Nevertheless enough of Cornell's captive-reared Peregrines now are established in the wild to expect that some will breed successfully in the wild within a few years.

Similar efforts, therefore, are being applied to Bald Eagles. Indeed, despite considerable controversy, other researchers now plan to begin a captive breeding and reintroduction program for California Condors in a desperate last effort to save these birds from extinction. Nobody knows, however, if the condor program will be successful because there are so few remaining birds, it is difficult to sex the birds, and there are other complications.

Various other adjunct captive breeding techniques also are being used to try to reverse declining reproductive rates or reproductive failures of endangered and rare birds of prey. One such technique is known as cross-fostering. This process involves putting captive-reared nestlings of one species into the nest of another species in order to allow the host parents to rear the nestlings. Thus some Cornell captive-reared Peregrines were placed in an active Prairie Falcon nest in the Snake River Birds of Prey Natural Area in Idaho. The Prairie Falcons accepted the nestling Peregrines and successfully cared for them. Cross-fostering, however, still is an experimental technique subject to careful examination because cross-fostered birds could develop abnormal or maladaptive behavior or sexual imprinting to the foster species rather than behavior typical of their own species. If such unacceptable problems do not develop, however, the technique could be used widely to reestablish breeding Peregrine Falcons throughout much of their former North American range. Some researchers, perhaps overly enthusiastic, now suggest that cross-

fostering also can be used to extend the range of some endangered species into areas never previously occupied, or to change the habits and habitat preferences of various populations of such species—creating entirely new lifestyles—that *the researchers* consider more adaptive to current world conditions. Unfortunately the ethical and moral ramifications of such drastic tamperings with millions of years of evolution and natural selection have received little, if any, serious consideration and debate. Should such drastic changes in a wild species be made if they are technically possible? Ornithologists and other concerned wildlife conservationists must consider such suggestions fully before using the techniques.

Another new raptor conservation technique, now used on Ospreys, involves the removal of some fertile eggs from nests in areas where normal hatching rates still occur and putting the eggs into the nests of other Ospreys in other areas which have experienced reproductive failures in recent year. This has resulted in some improvement in breeding success although reduced environmental levels of DDT also appear to be an important contributing factor to the better rates of Osprey production. Artificial insemination also is being used by some researchers to produce fertile eggs in some captive birds of prey.

At best, each of these techniques developed in recent years is an elaborate and expensive solution to severe environmental pollution and/or habitat destruction. In the future, with better controls of the pollutants entering the environment, such efforts may be unnecessary. As emergency interim measures, however, captive breeding projects and their related techniques are justified provided they are based upon sound scientific, conservation, and ethical standards. Some of the oppositon to such programs in the past developed because not all programs were justified or scientifically sound.

Educational Techniques

A wide variety of educational techniques is being used to inform and educate people concerning the ecological roles of birds of prey, their beauty, and their recreational values. Here are the most important of these educational techniques.

Magazines and Books

The oldest and most widely used method of informing people about birds of prey is with the use of good, well written magazine articles and books. Many such publications have been printed in the past and there continues to be a need for new material. In addition to the publication of such raptor literature, managers or directors of nature centers, hawk refuges, and other wildlife conservation facilities should make every possible effort to stock and offer for

175

sale publications featuring birds of prey. Those refuges which are established primarily to protect raptors and inform the public about them have particular obligations to offer a very wide selection of such literature to the public.

Teachers and school administrators also should make efforts to add raptor books to their school libraries and perhaps introduce such books into the classroom as texts. Good material is now available covering various aspects of the lives of birds of prey, and some of it can be used very effectively in the classroom. Similarly, Boy Scouts and Girl Scouts, 4-H groups, and similar organizations can make effective use of such literature in their natural history programs.

Newspapers

Countless articles dealing with birds of prey have appeared in the newspapers of the United States and Canada over the years and many more will continue to appear. The quality of such offerings ranges from excellent to poor. Raptor conservationists, therefore, should make special efforts to have local newspapers publish articles on these birds, provided the material is accurate and complete. Such articles can appear as regular news stories or in special outdoor or nature columns. When possible, photographs or drawings should accompany the articles.

Films and Slides

The use of 16-mm motion pictures and 35-mm slides, either on television or as lecture materials, also provides conservationists with exceptionally effective educational tools. Bird clubs, schools, and other concerned organizations all should try to include such audio-visual materials in their offerings. For example, my own 16-mm lecture film, "Hawks, Owls and Wildlife," has been shown to thousands of people in the East during the past ten years and many people doubtless have become more interested in birds of prey and their conservation because of seeing the film.

Television

The ability of television, either commercial or educational, to reach large viewing audiences and to influence their thinking suggests clearly that this medium should be used whenever possible to promote public understanding and appreciation of birds of prey. Although a few programs dealing with raptors already have appeared on television, it is clear that this medium has not been used to its full advantage. Specific efforts, therefore, should be made to try to develop new programs dealing with raptors. As in all such educational efforts, however, it is important that the materials used and the information presented be based upon sound scientific information.

Stamps

Commemorative postage stamps depicting birds of prey provide another way in which these birds can be brought to the public's attention. Many foreign countries already have shown raptors on their stamps. Until recently, however, few birds of prey appeared on United States commemorative postage stamps. Now this is beginning to change. Recently a California Condor, Great Horned Owl, Barred Owl, Great Gray Owl, and Saw-whet Owl each was featured on individual stamps. On January 18, 1978, the Canadian government issued a stamp with a Peregrine Falcon on it as part of a wildlife issue. Perhaps others will appear in the future.

The National Wildlife Federation has included some portraits of birds of prey on its wildlife conservation stamps, millions of which are distributed each year. Thus the public again is being exposed to some birds of prey. A special set of raptor stamps could be an even more worthwhile offering and doubtless would generate increased interest in birds of prey.

Commemorative postage stamps depicting birds of prey bring these birds to the attention of the general public and help to develop support for the conservation of these birds.   177

School Field Trips

In some parts of the United States and Canada science teachers in public and private schools include special teaching units on birds of prey in their curriculum and present such material with considerable success. Field trips designed to allow students to observe birds of prey often are part of these offerings.

In California, for example, some schools take their students on field trips to several well-known California Condor observation sites where they try to see one or more condors and also receive additional condor information from a National Audubon Society condor warden. Thus these students have firsthand opportunities to learn about one of the world's rarest birds, the problems it faces, and its prospects for survival.

Similarly some teachers in New Hampshire, Pennsylvania, Maryland, and elsewhere in close proximity to important hawk migration lookouts take students to the lookouts to observe and study autumn hawk migrations (or spring migrations in a few suitable areas). The students usually are required to fill in special field data sheets modified from those used by professional hawk researchers. Adequate classroom preparation before, and after, such field trips assures that the students understand the purpose of the field trip. Most students quickly learn to recognize general groups of birds such as accipiters, buteos, and falcons. A few students even become skilled hawk watchers and continue to visit the lookouts years after they were introduced to the topic in school.

Hunter Education

If the illegal shooting of birds of prey is to be eliminated, special efforts must be directed toward hunters to educate them in the ecological importance of these birds and their relationships with game species. Efforts at achieving this can include the preparation of leaflets to accompany all hunting licenses; lectures and seminars at sportsmen's organizations; posters; films; articles in hunting magazines; and special training courses for state and provincial wildlife officials. It is unlikely that these educational efforts will eliminate hawk and owl shooting entirely but they should stop most of it.

Eagle Weekends

In a few locations in the United States, special Bald Eagle viewing weekends are sponsored and operated by state parks to allow interested persons to see eagles and learn more about them. Two notable examples are at Lake Barkley State Resort Park in Kentucky and Reelfoot State Park in Tennessee. Naturalists provide controlled, guided tours of the areas and point out eagles to the participants. In addtion, special evening lectures also are provided at Reelfoot State Park along with a variety of other activities related to the eagles wintering in the area. Similarly, officials of Glacier National Park in Montana offer special Bald Eagle viewing opportunities at several sites within the park. Thousands of visitors come there every November to watch the birds. In all cases people are not allowed to approach the birds closer than about a quarter of a mile because eagles are extremely sensitive to human disturbance. However, from that distance there is no danger of disturbing the birds if the visitors are kept under proper control.

Conferences

Special regional, state, national, and international conferences at which raptor biologists, conservationists, and enthusiasts gather to present scientific papers, hold workshops, and exchange ideas and information about birds of prey and their conservation are extremely important. For example, in 1975 in Vienna, the World Conference on Birds of Prey produced major exchanges of ideas and information about raptors and their conservation, management, and protection. It also produced a series of important resolutions covering a wide spectrum of raptor-related topics. The purpose of these resolutions was to encourage concerned persons in various parts of the world to act upon many of the suggestions contained in the resolutions. Indeed, the published proceedings of that conference contain a wealth of pertinent information and ideas related to birds of prey and their welfare.

It is clear, therefore, that more conferences can act in more detail upon many of the ideas developed at the World Conference on Birds of Prey. Thus, Audubon groups, bird clubs, and others concerned with predatory birds should take the necessary steps to organize and hold their own raptor conferences in various states and provinces. Some important goals of such meetings would include careful examination of specific raptor problems in specific states and provinces, detailed discussions of such situations, and development of specific raptor conservation and management recommendations to be sent to the appropriate state and provincial wildlife officials. In some instances private persons or organizations also can act upon some of the recommendations of such conferences. The net result is a vital grass roots effort on behalf of birds of prey in many areas. In all cases, however, such recommendations should be based upon sound biological research and information.

A portion of the Kittatinny Ridge (in background) in Lehigh County, Pennsylvania. In 1978 the county executive issued an executive resolution designating the Lehigh County portion of the ridge as the Lehigh County Raptor Migration Area.

Resolutions

Although resolutions lack the force of law, and merely are suggestions, they nevertheless can be very useful public relations tools. The resolutions issued by the World Conference on Birds of Prey are cases in point. Similarly, the recent executive resolution issued by the county executive in Lehigh County, Pennsylvania, designating a Lehigh County Raptor Migration Area and calling to the public's attention the outstanding conservation-education opportunities available at the hawk lookouts in Lehigh County is another example of how such devices can benefit raptors by developing added public interest in seeing these birds.

Resolutions, therefore, should not be overlooked when promoting good will for birds of prey. They have not been used adequately in the past.

Exhibits

Still another technique that can be used effectively to develop better public understanding and appreciation of birds of prey is the preparation of exhibits for museums, nature centers, and schools. Such exhibits can feature various aspects of raptor biology, conservation, and ecology. Mounted specimens of various hawks and owls, photographs, maps, charts, and graphs all can be used as exhibit materials to develop or illustrate various topics or concepts. Generally, however, it is best to use a brief text and keep the scope of the information presented relatively simple. To try to include too much information in an exhibit can ruin the value of the overall effort.

EPILOGUE

As this book goes into type the Texas Parks and Wildlife Department issued a permit allowing for the airborne hunting of Golden Eagles and other predators. Several officials of the company receiving the permit have known links with past illegal shooting of Golden Eagles in the Southwest. The slaughter of Golden Eagles continues.

APPENDIX

RAPTOR CONSERVATION ORGANIZATIONS

A variety of conservation organizations now support protection and conservation of birds of prey in North America. Those listed here are especially concerned with this effort.

Eagle Valley Environmentalists, Inc.
P.O. Box 155
Apple River, Illinois 61001

Hawk Migration Association of
   North America
c/o Hawk Mountain Sanctuary
R. D. 2
Kempton, Pennsylvania 19529

Hawk Mountain Sanctuary
   Association
R. D. 2
Kempton, Pennsylvania 19529

International Council for Bird
   Preservation
c/o Smithsonian Institution
Washington, D. C. 20560

Macdonald Raptor Research Centre
McGill University
Ste. Anne de Bellevue, Quebec
   HOA 1CO
Canada

New Paltz Peregrine Falcon
   Foundation, Inc.
10 Joalyn Road
New Paltz, New York 12561

The Peregrine Fund
Cornell Laboratory of Ornithology
159 Sapsucker Woods Road
Ithaca, New York 14853

Raptor Information Center
National Wildlife Federation
1412 Sixteenth Street, N. W.
Washington, D. C. 20036

Raptor Research Foundation, Inc.
c/o Department of Zoology
Brigham Young University
Provo, Utah 84602

Society for the Preservation of
   Birds of Prey
Box 891
Pacific Palisades, California 90272

SELECTED
REFERENCES

American Ornithologists' Union
    1957   *Check-List of North American Birds.* Fifth Edition. Port
            City Press, Inc., Baltimore, Md.
Ames, P. L.
    1961   A Preliminary Report on a Colony of Ospreys. *Atlantic Nat-
            uralist,* 16: 26-33.
    1964   Notes on the Breeding Behavior of the Osprey. *Atlantic Nat-
            uralist,* 19: 15-27.
Ames, P. L. and G. S. Mersereau
    1964   Some Factors in the Decline of the Osprey in Connecticut.
            Auk, 81: 173-185.
Austing, G. R.
    1964   *The World of the Red-tailed Hawk.* J. B. Lippincott Co.,
            Philadelphia, Pa.
Austing, G. R. and J. B. Holt, Jr.
    1966   *The World of the Great Horned Owl.* J. B. Lippincott Co.,
            Philadelphia, Pa.
Bailey, B. H.
    1918   *The Raptorial Birds of Iowa.* Iowa Geological Survey, Des
            Moines, Ia.
Beck, H. H.
    1939   Mt. Johnson Island Eagle Sanctuary. *Bird-Lore,* 41 (4):
            222-224.
Bent, A. C.
    1937   *Life Histories of North American Birds of Prey.* Part 1. Bul-
            letin 167. U.S. National Museum, Washington, D.C.
    1938   *Life Histories of North American Birds of Prey.* Part 2.
            Bulletin 170. U.S. National Museum, Washington, D.C.

Bijleveld, M.
1974   *Birds of Prey in Europe.* Macmillan Press, Ltd., London.
Broun, M.
1949   *Hawks Aloft: The Story of Hawk Mountain.* Dodd, Mead Co., New York, N.Y.
Brown, L.
1970   *African Birds of Prey.* Houghton Mifflin Co., Boston, Mass.
Brown, L. and D. Amadon
1968   *Eagles, Hawks and Falcons of the World.* Two volumes. McGraw Hill Book Co., New York, N.Y.
Buckley, P.A.
1972   The Changing Seasons. *American Birds,* 26: 568-570.
California Condor Recovery Team
1974   *California Condor Recovery Plan.* U.S. Fish and Wildlife Service, Washington, D.C.
Chancellor, R. D. (Ed.)
1977   *World Conference on Birds of Prey: Report of Proceedings Vienna 1975.* International Council for Bird Preservation.
Choate, E. A.
1972   Spectacular Hawk Flight at Cape May Point, New Jersey on 16 October 1970. *Wilson Bulletin,* 84: 340-341.
1973   *The Dictionary of American Bird Names.* Gambit, Inc., Boston, Mass.
Clark, R. J.
1971   A Field Study of the Short-eared Owl (*Asio flammeus*) Pontoppidan, in North America. *Dissertation Abstracts International,* 31: No. 12.
Clark, W.S.
1974   Second Record of the Kestrel (*Falco tinnunculus*) for North America. *Auk,* 91: 172
Clay, W.M.
1953   Protective Coloration in the American Sparrow Hawk. *Wilson Bulletin,* 65: 129-134.
Craighead, J. J. and F. C. Craighead, Jr.
1940   Nesting Pigeon Hawks. *Wilson Bulletin,* 52: 241-248.
1956   *Hawks, Owls and Wildlife.* Stackpole Co., Harrisburg, Pa.
1966   Raptors. *In* Birds in Our Lives. U.S. Department of the Interior, Washington, D.C. Pp. 200-217.
Eisenmann, E.
1971   Range Expansion and Population Increase in North and Middle America of the White-tailed Kite (*Elanus leucurus*). *American Birds,* 25: 529-536.
Enderson, J. H.
1964   A Study of the Prairie Falcon in the Central Rocky Mountain Region. *Auk,* 81: 332-352.
Errington, P.L., F. Hamerstrom, and F.N. Hamerstrom, Jr.
1940   *The Great Horned Owl and its Prey in North-Central United States.* Research Bulletin 277. Agricultural Experiment Station, Iowa State College of Agriculture and Mechanic Arts, Ames, Ia.
Fisher, A. K.
1893   *The Hawks and Owls of the United States in their Relation to Agriculture.* Bulletin 3. Division of Ornithology and Mammalogy, U. S. Department of Agriculture, Washington, D.C.

Gabrielson, I. N. and F. C. Lincoln
1959   *Birds of Alaska*. Stackpole Co., Harrisburg, Pa., and Wild-
        life Management Institute, Washington, D.C.

Glazener, W. C.
1964   Note on the Feeding Habits of the Caracara in South Texas.
        Condor, 66: 162.

Graham, F., Jr.
1973   The Jury Is Still Out. *Audubon,* 75 (6): 69-75.

Greenway, J. C., Jr.
1958   *Extinct and Vanishing Birds of the World*. Special Publica-
        tion No. 13. American Committee for International Wild
        Life Protection, New York, N.Y.

Gross, A. O.
1931   Snowy Owl Migration 1930-31. *Auk,* 48: 501-511.
1947   Cyclic Invasions of the Snowy Owl and the Migration of
        1945-46. *Auk,* 64: 584-601.

Grossman, M. L. and J. Hamlet
1964   *Birds of Prey of the World*. Clarkson N. Potter, Inc., New
        York, N.Y.

Hamerstrom, F.
1972   *Birds of Prey of Wisconsin*. Department of Natural Re-
        sources, Madison, Wis.

Hammond, M. C. and C. J. Henry
1949   Success of Marsh Hawk Nests in North Dakota. *Auk,* 66:
        271-274.

Haugh, J.R.
1972   A Study of Hawk Migration in Eastern North America.
        Search, 2 (16): 1-60.

Hausman, L. A.
1928   *The Hawks of New Jersey and their Relation to Agriculture*.
        Bulletin 439. New Jersey Agricultural Experiment Station,
        New Brunswick, N.J.
1948   *Birds of Prey of Northeastern North America*. Rutgers Uni-
        versity Press, New Brunswick, N.J.

Heath, R. G., J. W. Spann, and J. F. Kreitzer
1969   Marked DDE Impairment of Mallard Reproduction in Con-
        trolled Studies. *Nature,* 224 (Oct. 4): 47-48.

Heintzelman, D. S.
1963   Bake Oven Hawk Flights. *Atlantic Naturalist,* 18: 154-158.
1964   Spring and Summer Sparrow Hawk Food Habits. *Wilson
        Bulletin,* 76: 323-330.
1966   Distribution and Population Density of Barn Owls in Lehigh
        and Northampton Counties, Pennsylvania. *Cassinia,* 49: 2-19.
1969a   Autumn Birds of Bake Oven Knob. *Cassinia,* 51: 11-32.
1969b   The Black Vulture in Pennsylvania. *Pennsylvania Game
        News,* 40 (5): 17-19.
1970a   Autumn Hawk Watch. *Frontiers,* 35 (1): 16-21.
1970b   The Hawks of New Jersey. Bulletin 13. New Jersey State
        Museum, Trenton, N.J.
1972a   *A Guide to Northeastern Hawk Watching*. Published pri-
        vately, Lambertville, N.J.
1972b   The Ospreys of Cedar Island. *Frontiers,* 36 (4): 8-11.
1975   *Autumn Hawk Flights: The Migrations in Eastern North
        America*. Rutgers University Press, New Brunswick, N.J.   185

1976   *A Guide to Eastern Hawk Watching.* Pennsylvania State
        University Press, University Park, Pa.

1979   *A Guide to Hawk Watching in North America.* Pennsylvania
        State University Press, University Park, Pa.

Heintzelman, D. S. and T. V. Armentano

1964   Autumn Bird Migration at Bake Oven Knob, Pa. *Cassinia,*
        48: 2-18.

Heintzelman, D. S. and A. C. Nagy

1968   Clutch Sizes, Hatchability Rates, and Sex Ratios of Sparrow
        Hawks in Eastern Pennsylvania. *Wilson Bulletin,* 80: 306-311.

Henny, C. J. and J. C. Ogden

1970   Estimated Status of Osprey Populations in the United States.
        J. Wildlife Management, 34: 214-217.

Henny, C. J. and H. M. Wright

1969   An Endangered Osprey Population: Estimates of Mortality
        and Production. *Auk,* 86: 188-198.

Herbert, R. A. and K. G. S. Herbert

1965   Behavior of Peregrine Falcons in the New York City Region.
        Auk, 82: 62-94.

Hickey, J. J.

1942   Eastern Population of the Duck Hawk. *Auk,* 59: 176-204.

1969   *Peregrine Falcon Populations: Their Biology and Decline.*
        University of Wisconsin Press, Madison, Wis.

Hickey, J. J. and D. W. Anderson

1968   Chlorinated Hydrocarbons and Eggshell Changes in Rap-
        torial and Fish Eating Birds. *Science,* 162: 271-273.

Holroyd, G. L. and J. G. Woods

1975   Migration of the Saw-whet Owl in Eastern North America.
        Bird-Banding, 46 (2): 101-105.

Hopkins, M., Jr.

1953   The Black Vulture as a Predator in Southern Georgia.
        Oriole, 18: 15-17.

Howard, H.

1945   *Fossil Birds.* Science Series No. 10, Paleontology No. 6. Los
        Angeles County Museum, Los Angeles, Calif.

Kaufmann, J. and H. Meng

1975   *Falcons Return.* William Morrow and Co., New York, N.Y.

Koford, C. B.

1953   *The California Condor.* National Audubon Society, New
        York, N.Y.

Lawrence, L. de K.

1949   Notes on Nesting Pigeon Hawks at Pimisi Bay, Ontario.
        Wilson Bulletin, 61: 15-25.

Ligon, J. D.

1963   Breeding Range Expansion of the Burrowing Owl in Flor-
        ida. *Auk,* 80: 367-368.

Mader, W. J.

1975   Biology of the Harris' Hawk in Southern Arizona. *Living
        Bird,* 14: 59-85.

May, J. B.

1935   *The Hawks of North America.* National Association of
        Audubon Societies, New York, N.Y.

McDowell, R. D. and L. A. Luttringer, Jr.
  1948   *Pennsylvania Birds of Prey*. Pennsylvania Game Commission, Harrisburg, Pa.

Melquist, W. E., D. R. Johnson, and W. D. Carrier
  1978   Migration Patterns of Northern Idaho and Eastern Washington Ospreys. *Bird-Banding*, 49: 234-236.

Meng, H.
  1959   Food Habits of Nesting Cooper's Hawks and Goshawks in New York and Pennsylvania. *Wilson Bulletin*, 71: 169-174.
  1971   The Swedish Goshawk Trap. *J. Wildlife Management*, 35: 832-835.

Munoff, J. A.
  1963   Food Habits, Growth, and Mortality in Nesting Marsh Hawks. *Kingbird*, 13: 67-74.

Oberholser, H. C.
  1974   *The Bird Life of Texas*. University of Texas Press, Austin, Tex.

Ogden, J. C.
  1974   The Short-tailed Hawk in Florida. I. Migration, Habitat, Hunting Techniques, and Food Habits. *Auk*, 91: 95-110.

Olendorff, R. R.
  1976   The Food Habits of North American Golden Eagles. *American Midland Naturalist*, 95 (1): 231-236.

Parkes, K. C.
  1966   Speculation on the Origin of Feathers. *Living Bird*, 5: 77-86.

Parmelee, D. F. and H. A. Stephens
  1964   Status of the Harris' Hawk in Kansas. *Condor*, 66: 443-445.

Payne, R. S.
  1962   How the Barn Owl Locates Prey by Hearing. *Living Bird*, 1: 151-159.

Peakall, D. B.
  1967a   Progress in Experiments on the Relation between Pesticides and Fertility. *Atlantic Naturalist*, 22: 109-111.
  1967b   Pesticide-induced Enzyme Breakdown of Steroids in Birds. *Nature*, 216 (5114): 505-506.

Peterson, R. T.
  1947   *A Field Guide to the Birds*. Second Revised and Enlarged Edition. Houghton Mifflin Co., Boston, Mass.
  1960   *A Field Guide to the Birds of Texas*. Houghton Mifflin Co., Boston, Mass.

Phillips, A., J. Marshall, and G. Monson
  1964   *The Birds of Arizona*. University of Arizona Press, Tucson, Ariz.

Phillips, R. E. and C. M. Kirkpatrick
  1964   *Hawks and Owls of Indiana*. Bulletin 8. Indiana Department of Conservation, Division of Fish and Game, Indianapolis, Ind.

Pinchon, P. R. and C. Vaurie
  1964   The Kestrel (*Falco tinnunculus*) in the New World. *Auk*, 78: 92-93.

Porter, R. D. and S. N. Weimeyer
  1969   Dieldrin and DDT: Effects on Sparrow Hawk Eggshells and Reproduction. *Science,* 165 (July 11): 199-200.

Postupalsky, S.
  1966a   Survey Osprey Nesting Success Wisconsin-Minnesota-Michigan.
  1966b   A Survey of Nesting Ospreys in Michigan—II. Unpublished Report.
  1968   The Status of the Osprey in the North-Central United States, 1967. Report from University of Michigan Biological Station.

Potter, J. K. and J. A. Gillespie
  1925   Observations on the Domestic Behavior of the Barn Owl Tyto Pratincola. *Auk,* 42: 177-192.

Ratcliffe, D. A.
  1967   Decrease in Eggshell Weight in Certain Birds of Prey. *Nature,* 215: 208-210.

Reed, J. H.
  1897   Notes on the American Barn Owl in Eastern Pennsylvania. *Auk,* 14: 374-383.

Reed, S. A.
  1959   An Analysis of 111 Pellets from the Short-eared Owl. *Jack-Pine Warbler,* 37: 19-23.

Reese, J. G.
  1970   Reproduction in a Chesapeake Bay Osprey Population. *Auk,* 87: 747-759.
  1972   A Chesapeake Barn Owl Population. *Auk,* 89: 106-114.

Reilly, E. M., Jr.
  1968   *The Audubon Illustrated Handbook of American Birds.* McGraw-Hill Book Co., New York, N.Y.

Robbins, C. S. *et al.*
  1966   *A Guide to Field Identification/Birds of North America.* Golden Press, New York, N.Y.

Rutzmoser, M. E. and D. S. Heintzelman
  1970   Peregrines and Pesticides/The Extinction of a Species. *Pennsylvania Game News,* 41 (6): 19-24.

Schaeffer, F. S.
  1968   A Unique Breeding Record: Saw-whet Owl. *EBBA News,* 31: 174-177.

Schmid, F. C.
  1966   The Status of the Osprey in Cape May County, New Jersey between 1939 and 1963. *Chesapeake Science,* 7 (4): 220-223.

Shick, C. S.
  1890   Birds Found Breeding on Seven Mile Beach, New Jersey. *Auk,* 7: 326-329.

Short, H. L. and L. C. Drew
  1962   Observations Concerning Behavior, Feeding, and Pellets of Short-eared Owls. *American Midland Naturalist,* 67: 424-433.

Spofford, W. R.
  1964   *The Golden Eagle in the Trans-Pecos and Edwards Plateau of Texas.* Audubon Conservation Report 1. National Audubon Society, New York, N.Y.
  1971   The Breeding Status of the Golden Eagle in the Appalachians. *American Birds,* 25: 3-7.

Sprunt, A., Jr.
1955   *North American Birds of Prey*. Harper & Brothers, New York, N.Y.

Stager, K. E.
1964   *The Role of Olfaction in Food Location by the Turkey Vulture* (Cathartes aura). Contributions Science 81. Los Angeles County Museum, Los Angeles, Calif.

Stewart, P. A.
1952   Dispersal, Breeding Behavior, and Longevity of Banded Barn Owls in North America. *Auk,* 69: 227-245.
1977   Migratory Movements and Mortality Rate of Turkey Vultures. *Bird-Banding,* 48 (2): 122-124.

Stieglitz, W. O. and R. L. Thompson
1967   *Status and Life History of the Everglade Kite in the United States.* Special Scientific Report—Wildlife No. 109: 1-21. U.S. Fish and Wildlife Service, Washington, D.C.

Stone, W.
1937   *Bird Studies at Old Cape May.* Two volumes. Delaware Valley Ornithological Club, Philadelphia, Pa.

Sutton, G. M.
1971   *High Arctic.* Paul S. Eriksson, New York, N.Y.

Sutton, G. M. and D. F. Parmelee
1956a   The Rough-legged Hawk in the American Arctic. *Arctic,* 9 (3): 202-207.
1956b   Breeding of the Snowy Owl in Southeastern Baffin Island. *Condor,* 58: 273-282.

Temple, S. A.
1972   Systematics and Evolution of the North American Merlins. *Auk,* 89: 325-338.

Van Tyne, J. and A. J. Berger
1959   *Fundamentals of Ornithology.* John Wiley & Sons, Inc., New York, N.Y.

Voous, K. H.
1977   Three Lines of Thought for Consideration and Eventual Action. *Proceedings World Conference on Birds of Prey,* pp. 343-347.

Wallace, G. J.
1948   *The Barn Owl in Michigan/Its Distribution, Natural History and Food Habits.* Technical Bulletin 208. Agricultural Experiment Station, Michigan State College, East Lansing, Mich.

Webster, H., Jr.
1944   A Survey of the Prairie Falcon in Colorado. *Auk,* 61: 609-616.

Wetmore, A.
1944   A New Terrestrial Vulture from the Upper Eocene Deposits of Wyoming. *Annals Carnegie Museum,* 30: 57-69.

Wilbur, S. R.
1978   *The California Condor, 1966-76.* North American Fauna, 72. U.S. Department of the Interior, Fish and Wildlife Service, Washington, D.C.

Willoughby, E. J. and T. J. Cade
1964   Breeding Behavior of the American Kestrel (Sparrow Hawk). *Living Bird,* 3: 75-96.

INDEX

ABOUT
THE AUTHOR

Donald S. Heintzelman has been an associate curator of natural science at the William Penn Memorial Museum and was for some years curator of ornithology at the New Jersey State Museum. A wildlife consultant, lecturer, and writer, he has traveled widely in North America, the West Indies, South America, the Falkland and Galapagos Islands, East Africa, and Antarctica photographing and studying wildlife. He is a wildlife film lecturer and was ornithologist on board the M.S. *Lindblad Explorer* on expeditions to Amazonia, Antarctica, and Galapágos. His books include *A Guide to Eastern Hawk Watching, A Guide to Hawk Watching in North America, Autumn Hawk Flights, The Hawks of New Jersey, North American Ducks, Geese & Swans, Finding Birds in Trinidad and Tobago*, and the forthcoming *A Guide to Bird Watching in the Americas.* Many of his notes and articles on ornithology, wildlife, and conservation have been published in leading national and international magazines.